The Long-Bell Story

By Jim Tweedie

In association with
The R. A. Long Historical Society

2-6-2015

Jim Tweedie

Param Press LLC
Lee's Summit, MO

Published by Param Press LLC
ParamPressLLC@gmail.com
Lee's Summit, MO 64081

In association with the R. A. Long Historical Society
www.ralonghistoricalsociety.org

Editor: Teresa Thornton Mitchell

Paperback Edition
ISBN -13: 978-0615920078
ISBN-10: 0615920071

Printed in the United States
First Edition – November 2014

Library of Congress Control Number: 2014955878

TABLE OF CONTENTS

ACKNOWLEDGEMENTS

Business formation in the late 1800's and early 1900's did not believe in saving important documents and certainly did not want to expose their business records to the general public. When Long-Bell merged with International Paper in 1956, company records were destroyed. Company papers that have become available are most generally held by individuals and tucked away in the attic or storage areas, forgotten over the years. Some of these documents have been donated to museums, for which we are most appreciative.

My research toward a document on The Long-Bell Lumber Company began in 1996 and focused on three valuable potential areas of discovery. The Cowlitz County Historical Museum, Kelso, Washington, The Longview Room, located in the "Merk" Building, Longview, Washington, and The Forest History Society, Durham, North Carolina. David Freece, Director Cowlitz County Historical Museum has been very supportive, allowing unfettered research through the Historical Society documents. Long-Bell "Logs", annual reports of Long-Bell and the complete report of S. E. Cronwall's financial analysis during Long-Bell's reorganization and back copies of the Longview Daily News were most important. The "Longview Room", organized by the late Clyde Shadiow and supported by John and Mary Chilson, owners of "The Merk", is a complete history of the formation of Longview and the surrounding communities. A set of "Long-Bell Logs" 1924 through 1956, had been donated and many pictures of mill activities and the early development of the town were available. In later years a complete series of back issues of the Longview Daily News, 1923 through the 1980's was also donated. Through the generosity of the Chilson's access to this valuable source was made available.

My third major source area was The Forest History Society, Durham, North Carolina and Archivist/ Librarian Cheryl Oakes. A wide variety of documents and publications from Long-Bell's early days helped form the beginnings of my research. Advice on where to find additional data was much appreciated. To these three major sources of information and assistance, my sincere thanks.

The search for data on Long-Bell was difficult due to the scattered base of information. Denise Morrison, Archivist, Science City Museum, Kansas City, Missouri was most helpful, Carol Riggs, Director Texas Forestry Museum, Lufkin , Texas, Chris Skaugset Director Longview Public Library, Karen Dennis and Susan Meyer Librarian, Longview Room, Longview Public Library, were all helpful, providing documents on Long-Bell activities. Thanks to the Tacoma Public Library's Northwest Room for access to The West Coast Lumberman, 1890's through 1940's, which carried accounts of Long-Bell lumber purchasing activities. The Special Collections Department, University Of Washington Libraries, Seattle, Washington, provided back issues of "The Timberman" magazine 1920 through 1950, which contained production volume and articles concerning Long-Bell and the lumber industry. Special thanks to J. M. Mc Clelland for his book, R. A. Long's Planned City, Lenore K. Bradley, for her book, Robert Alexander Long, International Paper, for permission to use of documents, papers and photographs, Weed Museum, Weed, California, Alford Linville, Curator and Sam Catalono former Long-Bell employees for assistance in understanding Weed activities, Siskiyou County Historical Society, Yreka, CA. publications from "The Siskiyou Pioneer".

A special thanks to Quinn Murk, Siletz, Oregon, for the loan of Long-Bell Director Meeting Notes 1907 through 1918 and Glen Comstock for the use of his vast library of Forest Products documents. The manuscript would not be complete without the proof reading and punctuation corrections by Ann Jordan, a retired English teacher and to George Miller for reading and commenting on organization and content, my thanks and appreciation for their assistance. The most notable experience of all the sources, was reading the Longview Daily News page by page from 1923 through 1948. What a great way to review history.

The Long-Bell Story does not dwell on the subject of Longview, Washington, although it is tightly connected with the move to the West by Long-Bell. The subject of building Longview and the saw mills has been thoroughly covered by John McClelland Jr. in the several books he wrote on the subject.

Without the assistance of The R. A. Long Historical Society and Teresa Mitchell editor, the book would not have been published, my thanks to them.

Jim Tweedie

ABOUT THE AUTHOR

James T. (Jim) Tweedie is a native of Longview, Washington and a 45 year veteran of the wood products industry. His grandparents came to Longview in 1924 as a result of Long-Bell's advertising campaign touting the new city and lumber operations. His parent soon followed, with father and grandfather employed at Long-Bell. An eighth grade teacher, Paul Anson arranged for class tours of Long-Bell's West Mill complex and Weyerhaeuser's pulp mill. The tours touched a nerve as Jim worked for both companies starting as a high school junior at the pulp mill working weekends and holidays.

After a tour of army duty in occupied Japan, the sawmill experience began in the spring of 1948, working weekends at Long-Bell's East Mill drop sorter. Seven years were spent at Long-Bell with experience gained at the east sawmill, planer and shipping departments. Lumber grading and shipping ocupied the majority of the time. The last year (1954 to 1955) was spent at Gardiner, Oregon supervising the dry shipping department.

The next 30 years was with Weyerhaeuser Company in a wide variety of assignments in lumber production and sales and marketing of lumber and plywood. A special time in his career was in Brussels, Belgium as manager of International Sales for softwood and hardwood plywood.

After retirement from Weyerhaeuser in 1984, he spent nine years as a export plywood broker, selling product into the European market, purchasing product from Southern Pine, West Coast and British Columbian sources, retiring for good in 1993.

Jim, a widower lives in University Place, Washington and is active in Plywood Pioneers and volunteer related activities. He is also active with the Cowlitz County Historical Society, contributing to their quarterly publications and involved with wood products historical research.

Jim Tweedie

INTRODUCTION

Little did Robert A. Long, Victor Bell and Robert White envision what the Long-Bell Lumber Company would become, when they formed their lumber business in 1875. The rapid growth of settlement throughout Kansas and Oklahoma and the opening of the Oklahoma Territory gave emphasis to Long-Bell's expansion. As railroads pushed tracks throughout the area, communities sprang up needing building supplies. Retail yards quickly followed with Long-Bell in the forefront. Discovery of oil and gas deposits spurred growth even further throughout the Southwestern portion of the United States.

Establishing retail yards, Long-Bell's core business, soon promoted the move toward acquiring production facilities to supply this rapidly growing business. Initially financing or taking partial ownership in established production facilities, Long-Bell always sought to control the sales of these mills. As Long-Bell grew, it soon controlled enough production to warrant establishment of a wholesale selling function to move the excess production not needed by the retail chain. Growth continued spurred on by a loyal cadre of associates who had joined Long-Bell. Robert A. Long, General Manager of the existing company was a shrewd judge of character, picking his associates with care. By 1900 the management team would remain stable, with few exceptions throughout the life of Long-Bell.

By the late 1890's and early 1900's Long-Bell was on solid ground, ready to expand from Arkansas and Oklahoma Territory into Louisiana and Texas. Building Mills at Bon Ami, Longville and De Ridder, mills were purchased at Yellow Pine, Woodworth, Ludington and Lake Charles in Louisiana, Pine Bluff, Arkansas, Lufkin and Doucette, Texas. In 1917 a mill was acquired at Quitman, Mississippi ending the expansion in the south. Long-Bell was one of the dominant lumber companies in the south.

With each new mill came growth in the wholesale selling activities of Long-Bell. From starts with The Sabine Valley Lumber Company, Texarkana, Arkansas in 1885, the selling function grew to forty salesmen by the late teens. A purchasing office was established in Tacoma, Washington in 1896 and purchased shingles and western lumber products until 1912 averaging 1600 carloads a year. Treated products were added by 1916, specializing in fence posts, poles and piling. Railroad ties and other products soon introduced. Sash and doors, Hardwoods and export sales functions soon added to their success.

In 1903 Long-Bell began investing in The Weed Lumber Company, Weed, California a producer of Ponderosa and Sugar Pine Lumber, Sash and doors, giving them long term source of production. Through continued investment over several years, controlling interest in the company was obtained by 1916. Due to previous sales agreements, Long-Bell could not control the sash and door segment until the early 1920's but welcomed the opportunity when control was gained on sales. By 1920, Long-Bell would become the largest lumber company, in the United States, surpassed only by the Weyerhaeuser group of companies who sold through a mutual sales company.

Long-Bell viewed many opportunities to expand and ventures were established in owning coal properties in from 1900 to 1912, selling cutover land for small farms in mid teens, leasing cutover land for gas and oil exploration, building wooden ships during World War and production of Navel Stores from company timberland. Some were profitable, others were not.

In 1918, Long-Bell was faced with depleted timber holdings and faced dissolution without a major move west. Timber sources were non- existent in the south. The decision was made to move west and a large block of timber purchased in Southwest Washington, and the largest mill system in the world was erected at Longview, Washington. Two mills were built with one opening in 1924 and the second in 1926. With the building of the mills, a new community was also built to house the employees. This would lead to an eventual re-organization of the company due to its enormous cost.

The 1930's depression hit Long-Bell hard. Overproduction by the industry accelerated the downward slide of price levels for lumber. Long-Bell financed itself by selling industrial bonds, and declining sales revenue drove Long-Bell to receivership by 1934. The company vowed that every cent would be paid and it took from 1935 until March, 1944 to recover and Long-Bell was able to accumulate capital allowing it to purchase timber and other producing units, extending the life of the company until merger with International Paper in 1956.

Robert A. Long

CHAPTER 1

THE COMPANY

From the modest beginnings of the company formed April 30, 1875, the founder's, R. A. Long, Victor Bell and Robert White could not envision the rapid growth and eventual stature that the Long-Bell Lumber Company would achieve. R. A. Long and his partners formed the R. A. Long Company as a result of a failed venture in selling hay at Columbus, Kansas in 1874. With a loan and encouragement from his uncle, Churchill J. White, head of Kansas City Savings Bank, Kansas City, Missouri, R. A. Long, Robert White and Victor Bell purchased a carload of lumber to cover the hay and found that selling the lumber brought a greater return than the hay. Purchasers of the lumber encouraged them to enter the retail lumber business as the only retail yard in town was known to be expensive and unreliable. In 1875 R. A. Long & Company was formed, opening up a retail yard in Columbus, Kansas. (1) The company grew rapidly, adding retail yards in Kansas and in the Oklahoma and Indian territories as railroads extended their tracks throughout the Southwest portion of the United States. Investments in existing sawmills began by the late 1880's located in Western Arkansas.

R. A. Long and Company entered the retail lumber business and subsequently lumber manufacturing at exactly the right time. The railroad expansion, gas and oil development and the opening of the Oklahoma and Indian Territories led to building towns and communities throughout the Southwest. Developing communities demanded building materials, which led Long-Bell and other competitors to expand.

With the formation of R. A. Long and Company, R. A. Long would be the only active participant, as Robert White returned to clerking at the Kansas City Savings Bank and Victor Bell left for Harvard University. R. A. Long returned to Columbus, Kansas and on April 30, 1875 unloaded the first carload of lumber purchased by the new company. For the next two years, he would be the manager, laborer, accountant and chief clerk. The company flourished and business was brisk. In 1877, S. H. (Sam) Wilson joined R. A. Long and would become a mentor and loyal lieutenant. The company began to grow, adding a yard at Emporia Kansas, followed by additions each year and by 1879 the company consisted of six retail yards. (2)

In 1877 Robert White, a cousin of R. A. Long, died and his interest was purchased by the remaining partners. In 1884, with the company thriving, they dissolved the partnership and incorporated as Long-Bell Lumber Company, in the state of Missouri, with Victor Bell, President and R. A. Long, General Manager. Victor Bell would retire from active management of the company in 1885, exchanging his stock for preferred shares in the company. (3)

R. A. Long surrounded himself with many key managers in the building of the company. S. H. (Sam) Wilson was a brother in law of R.A. Long, who took over management of the retail yard chain. He would be named Vice President and assistant General Manager in 1899 and would remain in this capacity until 1903, when he died. C.D. Morris, another brother in law, who had previous experience in the industry joined the company in 1880, was placed in charge of wholesale sales. In 1898 Morris joined King Ryder Lumber Company as Secretary and sales manager, retiring in the early 1900's due to ill health. C. B. Sweet, previously an intense retail yard competitor of Long-Bell in Kansas, joined Long-Bell in 1897 as manager of Hudson River Lumber Company, Hudson, Arkansas. The chain of retail yards known as C. B. Sweet and Brothers was absorbed into The Long-Bell Lumber Company. Upon the death of S. H. (Sam) Wilson in 1903, Sweet became Vice President and Manufacturing Manager for Long-Bell, with prime responsibility for manufacturing and timber lands. This appointment affected all of the affiliated companies. At that time Sweet was also elected as a director of Long-Bell, retiring in 1914. (4)

C. B. Sweet

There were other key members of the original management team. M. B. (Mike) Nelson joined Long-Bell in 1898 as superintendent of the wholesale division (Sabine Valley Lumber Company). He became Vice President, General Sales Manager and Director in 1904, President in 1923, following the resignation of F. J. Bannister and retired in 1948. J. H. Foresman joined the company in1898, working in the retail yard system, advancing to manager of retail yards on the death of S. H. Wilson, was elected a director in 1903 and Vice President in 1914 and served until 1932. William F. Ryder, the longest serving employee from the early years, joined the company in 1881, at Opolis, Kansas, moving to several other yards until 1890 when he was put in charge of the Antlers Indian Territory mill until 1894. In 1896 he was in charge with W. S. King of the

Thomasville, Indian Territory saw mill operation. In later years W. F. Ryder would be involved with searching for timber throughout the South and deeply involved in the Washington timber acquisition with the logging town of Ryderwood named after him.

B. H. Smith joined Long-Bell as Treasurer of Pacific Coast Lumber and Supply, Kansas City, Missouri, a Long-Bell subsidiary. In 1895 he became manager of Sabine Valley Lumber Company, Texarkana, Arkansas, a wholesale operation for Long-Bell moving in 1898 to Thomasville, Indian Territory as Vice President and General Manager. When the Bon Ami mill was built, he became general manager and remained in that position until 1913 when he resigned due to ill health. (5) In later years Smith would return to Long-Bell as a salesman at Sacramento, California until retiring in 1947. He would become the second 50 year employee after R. A. Long. This group of long term employees served 40 to 50 years as well as being major investors in the company.

The next generation of management entered the company in the late 1890's and early 1900's and would remain with Long-Bell the rest of their working lives. Several of these key people were second generation employees, sons or sons in law of the original management team. J. D. Tennant, son in law of C. B. Sweet, joined the company in 1900. He worked at the mill level, managed a retail yard for a short period and returned to Calcaiseu Lumber Company, Lake Charles, Louisiana, as Order clerk,then on to Hudson River Lumber Company, DeRidder, Louisiana as mill superintendent in 1907. In 1911 he became assistant to the Vice President of Manufacturing. Upon the retirement of C. B. Sweet, he was elected as a Director and General Manager of Manufacturing. In 1920, Tennant was elected as a Vice President, taking charge of the Western development. S. M. Morris started with Long-Bell in 1893, proofing inventory books at Kansas City, Missouri as a schoolboy. In 1900 Morris was employed at the Thomasville, Indian Territory mill, working various jobs, he was the son of C. D. Morris. After working at Thomasville and Bon Ami mills, spent a year in the retail yard system at Enid and Newkirk, Oklahoma. Morris was promoted to General Manager at Lufkin, Texas, where he remained for 17 years. Morris was selected as General Western Manager, supervising the building of the Longview complex and elected a Director and Vice President in 1922, remaining in Longview for the rest of his career, retiring with 53 years of service.

Jesse Andrews, General Counsel represented the company since 1912, becoming a Director in 1922 and a key member of the financial re-structuring committee in the mid 1930's. R. F. Morse joined the company in 1906 at Calcaiseu Lumber Company, Lake Charles, Louisiana. Morse was responsible for creating the Export Department in 1911, becoming General Manager at Ludington, Louisiana in 1913 and in 1918 he became manager at Quitman, Mississippi. Morse transferred to Longview, taking part in the development and management of the Longview

Division, later becoming manager of Western Timberlands, becoming a Vice President in 1947. L. L. Chipman joined Long-Bell with the purchase of Fidelity Land and Improvement Company, working in Coal sales. He became head of Export Sales in 1913 and served in that role until 1934, when it was absorbed into the general sales function. Selected as General Manager of Southern Production in the late 1930's and early 1940's, L. L. Chipman retired in 1948 as a 50 year employee. A. B. Everitt, Vice President and General Manager of the Retail Yard system, joined Long-Bell in 1897, as a teamster delivering coal. He managed retail yards, eventually becoming Division Manager of the Enid, Oklahoma area. In 1923, became Assistant General Manager of the retail system and in 1932 upon J. F. Foresman's passing, became General Manager, retiring in 1948 with 51 years of service. J. M. White, General Manager, Weed, California from 1917 until 1947, was elected President of Long-Bell in 1948. White joined Weed Lumber Company in 1906. (6) This outstanding group of leaders had over 370 years of management experience with The Long-Bell Lumber Company. All had been given responsible positions at a young age. R. A. Long had an exceptional eye for selecting the individuals who would run the company.

Long-Bell invested in many ventures from the beginnings of the company. Seldom did they own a company outright, choosing to buy a controlling interest in the venture. The financial statement of The Long-Bell Company, January 1, 1921 for the year 1920 lists the investment in the various companies under the Long-Bell umbrella, showing the percentage owned by Long-Bell.

Calcasieu Longleaf Lumber Company	82.725 %
Hudson River Lumber Company	86.289 %
King/ Ryder Lumber Company	78.758 %
Long-Bell Lumber Company (Quitman)	69.880 %
Longville Lumber Company	81.089 %
Ludington Lumber Company	71.986 %
Rapides Lumber Company	81.346 %
Long-Bell Farm Land Company	9.7 %
Long-Bell Lumber Company of Texas	100.0 %
(Texas and New Mexico Retail Yards)	
Long-Bell White Pine Lumber Company	100.0 %
(Reservation Tract of Ponderosa Pine Timber in Oregon)	

The Globe Lumber Company Inc.	84.255 %
Weed Lumber Company	59.342 %
Louisiana Pacific Railway Company	90.169 %
The Sibley Lake Bistineau Central Railway Company	83.000 %
The Woodworth @ Louisiana Central Ray Company	60.000 %

Not listed in the above were the following companies associated with Long-Bell, Minnetonka Lumber Company, Long-Bell Naval Stores, Calcasieu Mercantile Company, Arkansas Short Leaf Lumber Company and Fidelity Lumber Company. Most of these would be 100 % owned. In virtually every instance where Long-Bell was involved in a venture, a new company was formed. Minority stockholders of all the combined companies held 30% of the stockholders investment. (7)

Throughout Long-Bell history, attempts to consolidate the various companies into one entity were made. Director notes of 1908 and 1914 indicate efforts toward consolidation. With the move to the West, it was felt necessary to consolidate the company under one name. As a result of exchanging stock of the subsidiary companies for stock in the parent company the consolidation was completed. This was accomplished in 1922, with all subsidiary companies becoming divisions of the parent company, with the exception of Weed Lumber Company and Quitman, Mississippi where complete ownership had not been achieved. The Weed Lumber Company became a division of Long-Bell in 1926 when Long-Bell purchased the remaining stock. The Quitman mill was absorbed into Long-Bell as a division in the mid 1920's.

With the formation of The Long-Bell Lumber Company in 1884, under Missouri laws, Victor Bell was elected president and R. A. Long was named General Manager. This arrangement remained in effect until Victor Bell retired from the company in 1895. R. A. Long was elected to the presidency and filled the position until February, 1921 when he was elected as Chairman of the company. F. J. Bannister succeeded R. A. Long, having previously served as Secretary of the company. In August 1923, F. J. Bannister resigned as president; but retained his position as a director of the company. F. J. Bannister would become the only defection from senior management ranks, other than several leading sales executives who moved on to other venues. He was succeeded by M. B. Nelson, who had been General Sales Manager of the company since 1904 and a vice president since 1914. M. B. Nelson would serve as president until 1948, through some of the most troubling times for the company and some of the most rewarding years, recording record profits and expansion. J. M. White, General Manager of the Weed complex was named president in April 1948, serving through the rest of Long-Bell's years. In the 81 years of existence as Long-Bell, the company had four presidents and one chairman, all who spent their working life in dedicated employment with Long-Bell.

The Long-Bell Board of Directors was made up of company employees, with the exception of occasional outside legal counsel throughout the life of the company, except for the period during 1934 through 1942, when the company was under the control of court ordered reorganization. Board membership consisted of five members to a high of eighteen. Board composition was normally represented by major department heads such as retail yards, manufacturing, sales and general office management. As the company grew larger, board members would represent several areas within a segment of responsibility. There was always diversity within their discussions, but there was only one arbitrator, in the presence of R. A. Long. In the early years, C. B. Sweet, a major stockholder in the company was often the decision maker in the absence of R. A. Long.

With the rapid expansion of production, Long-Bell began to have a wider profile in the American lumber scene. In 1899, the company shipped 170 million board feet of lumber, with production of 135 million and purchases of 35 million feet. By 1915, production was up to 500 million board feet of Southern Pine and Hardwood lumber. Long-Bell would be the second largest producer of Hardwood lumber in the United States. The high point in company production was 1925, with 12 mills and a capacity of 800 million board feet, although fires at Pine Bluff, Arkansas in 1921 and Longville, Louisiana in 1922 did reduce the volume potential. Long-Bell would become one of the two largest lumber companies in the country.

When the company was incorporated, the capitalization was set at $300,000. It increased in 1891 to $1,000,000 and in 1902 increased again to $1,250,000.   In developing his company, R. A. Long utilized borrowed funds extensively, so the early successes of the company bode well for repeated requests for funds as the retail yards and manufacturing units generated large amounts of cash to repay loans and build a surplus of funds. Even with favorable payment records, Long-Bell chose to use credit or industrial bonds to finance day to day operations and expansions. In April, 1907 the Long-Bell Board of Directors voted to increase capitalization from $ 1,250,000 dollars to $ 10 million dollars. The method of financing was through issuance of general obligation bonds. As soon as a certificate was issued authorizing the increase, a stock dividend in the form of company shares would be issued to shareholders of record from existing company surplus, this seemed to be a regular practice, when issuing bonds. In 1910, the company again increased capitalization to $13 million, in 1921 to $25 million and in 1922 to $ 30 million dollars, signifying rapid growth in all sectors of the company. (8)

M. B. Nelson
50 Years

J. M. White
President

In 1918, the time had come to decide whether the company was to liquidate, having cut most of their available Southern timber. With only a few years of timber left to cut, the decision had to be made on the next course of action. Other than R. A. Long, who was 67 at the time, the key managers were forty to fifty years of age. R. A. Long felt that he needed a consensus of opinion on what the next steps for the company should be, so he, Mr. Long convened a meeting of all key managers and directors, including their wives to discuss the future. In the ensuing discussion, the entire group voted to move to the West. R. A. Long invited the wives because he wanted them to be aware that many of their husbands would spend considerable time away from home. With the conclusion of the meeting, the search was on to find timber and a new location for the renewed growth of the company. (9)

Financial panics in 1907 and 1912 caused the company to rein in their aggressive approach for expansion. Crop failures, reduction in gas and oil exploration and general business conditions often caused Long-Bell management periods of concern. Pressure to enact credit collections was expressed to all retail yard managers and wholesale accounts. Constant attention to cash positions to insure enough funds to pay off pending bond maturities and current obligations were often the subject for discussion at Board of Director meetings. R. A. Long and his senior managers were not afraid to take substantial risks. The combined annual statement of January 1, 1921 lists a stockholder investment of $ 40,498 075.93. Included in the liabilities was $12,295,081.72 in notes payable, accounts payable, commercial paper, accrued expenses and income taxes. In addition $4,447,633.00 of timber mortgage notes on Southern plants, plus $ 16,002,666.68 of timber purchase contracts in Oregon and Washington. (10) This was a tremendous risk when looking at building a major facility in the west with unknown costs to be determined. Their financial situation in the mid 1930's is well documented and despite their travails, the company did recover and continued to grow once World War II was over.

Another innovation Long-Bell management sponsored was selling stock to the employees. On April 6, 1925 Long-Bell offered class B stock for sale to all employees with limits of stock for purchase set based upon wages or salary received. Employees had until April 18, 1925 to apply for stock purchase. Foreman and department heads explained the plan to employees, making sure they understood that this was a voluntary program and that the company took no position on the matter. At the end of subscription, 3,972 employees had signed up to purchase 29,406 shares of stock. The price paid was the open market level at time of purchase at an average price of $49.86. Arrangements were made to make payments on an easy pay plan, so as not to place a major burden on the employees. In April 1928, an update on the stock purchase program was reported in "The Long-Bell Log". Stock certificates were issued to 2,389 employees for 20,816 shares of stock. For 34 months purchasers of stock had been paying an average of $11.29 per month into the stock fund for a total of $917,070.26. (11)

The company was formed when accounting and business practices were rudimentary and accomplished significant results even though few of the initial management possessed formal or business education. Production and sales reports were detailed and frequent, allowing management the ability to monitor results. The company would be in the forefront of modern devices, such as installing the first national private wire printer and telegraph system in the nation in 1926. Orders could be wired to the mills when needing special service, with a rail car number returned the same day.

As we review Long-Bell's impressive history, the company ranks high in helping the nation grow through providing quality products for homes and communities. Expanding as the nation grew, they were in the forefront in providing product to meet the challenges national growth required.

F. J. Bannister

References :

(1)   Robert Alexander Long, A Lumberman of the Gilded Age, Lenore K. Bradley, Page 20

(2)   A Great Business Organization, American Lumberman, April 21, 1900, Page 1

(3)   Robert Alexander Long, A Lumberman of the Gilded Age, Lenore K. Bradley, Page 27

(4)   From Tree To Trade in Yellow Pine, American Lumberman, July2,1904, Page 54

(5)   From Tree To Trade in Yellow Pine, American Lumberman, July2, 1904, Page 74

(6)   Long-Bell Log, May, 1948, Page 8

(7)   Financial Statement of The Long-Bell Lumber Company, January 1, 1921, Exhibit # 3
        Invest ment in Associated Companies

(8)   Long-Bell Log, April 1925, Page 30

(9)   Robert Alexander Long, A Lumberman of the Gilded Age, Lenore K. Bradley, Page 74

(10)   Financial Statement of The Long-Bell Lumber Company and Associated Companies
        January 1, 1921   Liabilities and Exhibit # 5 Timber Mortgage Notes and Exhibit # 6
        Timber Purchase Contracts, Oregon and Washington

(11)   Long-Bell Log , May 1925, Page 2 and 3 and April 1928 Page 7

Okeene, O. T.

Pond Creek, O. T.

Renfrow, O. T.

Wakita, O. T.

Waukomis, O. T.

Baxter, Kan.

Bolton, Kan.

Chanute, Kan.

Chautauqua, Kan.

Cherokee, Kan.

MISCELLANEOUS VIEWS OF THE RETAIL YARDS OF THE LONG-BELL LUMBER COMPANY.

14

Chapter 2

RETAIL YARDS

The establishment of the first retail yard at Columbus, Kansas in 1875 was the foundation for the development of the company known as Long-Bell. R. A. Long could not imagine what would follow in the ensuing 80 years. Lumber retail yards were one of main driving forces in the development of the central plains and southwest sections of our country. As the railroad network expanded across the central and southwestern states and territories, new settlements sprung up behind them. The railroads were very aggressive in promoting these expansions in order to generate revenue. There were thousands of retail yards springing up across the nation. In the central United States, chains of retail yards were established. Peavy Yards, Emmer Brothers, Thompson Yards (Weyerhaeuser), T. W. Hager and Central Yards, all operated in Nebraska, Montana, Minnesota, Michigan, the Dakota's and Iowa. Ownership ran from 75 to over 100 individual yards per ownership. Long-Bell, Sutherland, Foster, Foxworth- Galbraith and others were active in Kansas, Texas, Oklahoma and Missouri.

The retail yards of the late 1900's and up to the mid 20th century operated much like Lowe's and Home Depot do today. They attempted to stock everything a builder would need for construction. As home building became more sophisticated, the services provided by the retail yards expanded greatly. In addition to building products, coal, hay and grain were carried in most locations. As communities grew, additional retail yards would open up to capture the added business. Often major competitors would be located in the same community.

The growth of population across the central and southwestern sections of the country led to a sophistication of the retail trade adding sash and doors, paint, windows and home plans to services offered. In addition to lumber products, cedar shingles (major roofing product), treated products, hardware, glass, tools, nails, paint and cement all increased in volume. Then as now, quality and dependable service were important to the retail yard.

Long-Bell opened their first yard in Columbus, Kansas in 1875, adding new yards as opportunities were presented. In 1877, the company owned seven yards all located in Kansas. Also in

1877 Robert White had died and R.A. Long and Victor Bell purchased his interest in the company.

By 1883, 14 yards were operating under the Long-Bell name. Continued growth moved the company to set up a purchasing division to buy material for the yards. In 1901, 20 new yards were opened in Oklahoma and Indian Territory under the Minnetonka Lumber Company name. (1)

Long-Bell was constantly looking to add retail yards to its existing chain. A retail company Brown Supply was added in the early 1900s and Alfalfa Lumber Company which operated in Texas. In 1905 Botts Lumber Company, Wichita, Kansas was added consisting of twelve yards in Kansas and Oklahoma. (2) By 1904 61 yards were operating spurred on by the rapidly expanding oil and gas boom. 1906 saw 95 yards throughout Oklahoma, Kansas, Texas and the Indian Territory. By 1909, Long-Bell retail yards, employed 229 men, had 172 horses, 50 wagons, carrying 25 million feet of lumber in inventory. In that year they sold,43.5 million feet of lumber, 47,500 million shingles,1.5 million feet of battens, 2.5 million feet of moulding, 25.000 barrels of lime, 12.000 barrels of cement, 21.5million pounds of coal, 7.413 million pounds of cement plaster, 27,000 windows and 24,000 doors, a sizeable jump, from the first yard. (3) By 1919, Long-Bell and affiliated yards were the larg-est retail yard chain in the nation with 121 yards having added the York-Key, a Woodward, Oklahoma chain.

Population growth spurred the expansion of the retail chain. The opening of the Oklahoma and Indian Territories was the spark for rapid growth by Long-Bell. Lumber sales in 1918 through the retail system, was 72 million board feet. Inventory levels in the retail chain averaged 45 million board feet, occasionally increasing to 55 million board feet. At this point, Long-Bell was the country's largest lumber company, with sales of $43,609 million in wholesale and retail categories. This was a substantial increase from 1904, when $7.2 million in sales was recorded. Company employment in 1919 was 3713. Oklahoma and Kansas were the principal growth areas for Long-Bell.

Management of the retail yards became the responsibility of Samuel H. Wilson, brother-in-law of R. A. Long, who had joined the company in 1877. S. H. Wilson was instrumental in developing the growth of the retail system and became Vice President and Assistant General Manager of Long-Bell in 1894. He served in this role until he died in 1903. (4) S. H. Wilson was followed by Joseph H. Foresman who began working for Long-Bell in 1889 and served as Vice President and Director until he died in 1932. He was replaced by A. B. Everitt, as Vice President and General Manager of the retail system until he retired in 1948. Long-Bell had excellent management of their retail system through-out the company history.

When considering the history of Long-Bell, it should be noted, that few of its management personnel had formal education. The key to company success was the development of its employees into successful managers through hard work, responsibility and trust. In developing managers at its many locations, individuals charged with the operation of a retail yard became bookkeepers, yardmen and managers, all in one. Most, if not all of the managers who rose to senior positions, started in the retail yard system.

It is interesting to note, that despite the difficulty of travel throughout the rural southwest, personnel moved from yard to yard within the Long-Bell system. The career path usually followed was from laborer, assistant manager then to manager. A manager might serve at several locations, each move accepting more responsibility and a larger yard. Management talent was often very young, 20 to 25, experienced in the retail business, having entered the work force at 15/16 years of age or younger. Many of the retail yard managers stayed with Long-Bell their entire career.

J. H. Foresman - AML 1-11-08

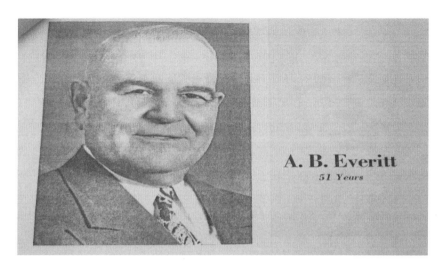

A. B. Everitt
51 Years

Despite R. A. Long's lack of formal education, he was well versed in the need for information, whether retail yard, production or wholesale sales. The knowledge of business conditions, inventory levels, status of accounts receivable and other factors were all important to the day to day operations of the business. With the lack of fast communications, reports were limited to mail delivery, on a monthly basis. Many of the reports required were based on experience developed over the years. Effort was made to keep the process simple but effective. The yards would use a carbon paper order set for the monthly reports, which contained a complete listing of credit and cash sales, cash receipts and payouts, outstanding accounts, daily bank balances, general office account, expense account, estimated profit for the day and total sales month to date. The status of each category was balanced by month and year. (5)Throughout Long-Bell's long history, economic periods of distress occurred. In the early 1900's, again in 1912 to 1914, after World War I and the depression of the 1930's were periods of severe economic distress. The retail yard manager was responsible for collecting for sales made in addition to his other duties. Constant reminders and pressure from R. A. Long and the Board of Directors to press for collections were part of the daily routine.

Reviewing these details allowed management to keep a hand on the pulse of the business. In addition to the information required, the yards recorded all incoming stock for reference and auditor use. Yards were required to keep a log on business completed and local market conditions. Accounts receivable data by customer, date of first and last purchase and address and occupation of debtor were recorded. Reports of stock received, car number, condition of arrival and quality were also kept. With this type of detailed information, the general office was able to develop a complete statement, showing sales by yard, profit and supply source, expenses, net gain and quantity of sales by item. It is interesting to note that the competing line yards used the same type of information.

The retail yards were the main profit source for the first 25 years of the company's existence, prior to entry into the wholesale market and for many years after. The yards were constantly looking for new and better products to sell. With an expanding company, opportunities for new products came with the acquisition of controlling interest in Weed Lumber Company, Weed, California, opening up opportunities for sash, doors and window parts. A treating plant was opened at Shreveport, LA., with treated lumber, posts piling and paving blocks in 1916.Coal being the standard heating fuel was sold in the retail yards from the beginning. Fidelity Land and Coal was added to Long-Bell holdings as early as 1903 with 6 mines located in Kansas, Missouri and Arkansas. Hardwood lumber was added in 1911 with the major item being Oak Flooring. All of these products contributed greatly to the retail yard profit.

Retail yards, were not originally planned to operate as a major outlet for manufacturing side of the business, taking only 5 to10% of the annual production. Retail yard requirements of lumber were purchased on the outside and used supply from company mills only when surplus stocks were being developed in slow markets, or when it could be purchased at a lower price. Long-Bell operated a purchasing office in Tacoma, Washington from 1894 through 1912, and had a concentration yard in Tacoma, Washington at 16th and California Avenue, for Cedar Shingles. It was reported in the West Coast Lumberman Journal that Long-Bell purchased an average of 1600 carloads a year during this time period.(6)

The trend in the volume of business through the retail yards is shown by summary of lumber purchased from 1928 through six months of 1932. The purchases show that Southern Pine recaptured many markets, due to much lower freight rates from southern mills.(7)

	1928	1929	1930	1931	1932
Pine	15,364	15,019	11,201	9,223	2,208
Fir	24,403	20,240	8,579	3,312	782
Pon.	5,474	5,612	2,346	1,426	460
Tot.	45,241	40,871	22,126	13,961	3,450

Volumes are in millions of board feet

Carloads of Lumber Purchased

| 1,967 | 1,777 | 962 | 607 | 150 |

Miscellaneous carloads purchased (Cement, Nails, etc.)

| 501 | 434 | 275 | 149 | 49 |

With the explosive growth in settlement of Oklahoma and the Indian Territories (later to become the state of Oklahoma) yard expansion was necessary to keep up with the influx of immigration. The following chart illustrates the pattern of growth in the Long-Bell retail yard system.

	Yards	Kan.	Okl.		Mis.	Tex.	N.M	Ar.	Or.	Wa.
1904	62	25	31 ot	6 it						
1921	128	26	92		3	5	1			
1943	79	17	50		2	4	1		3	2
1951*	111	21	60		10	4	1	3	4	6
1954*	107	23	58		9	5	1	3	3	5
1955*	100	21	54		9	5	1	3	3	3
1956	114	22	65		4	5	1	5	5	7

*During these three years, one yard in Colorado and one yard in California. 1904 OT (Oklahoma Territory), IT (Indian Territory).

With the decision to take over the sales of windows and doors from Weed Lumber Company management, distribution facilities were opened up in the early 1920's at Enid, McAlester and Oklahoma City, Oklahoma and Amarillo, Texas. These facilities could deliver windows and doors to surrounding retail yards quickly which added another service.

With the catastrophic depression in 1929, lumber and related business ground to a halt.

Long-Bell forced into a re-organization in 1932 began to curtail the size of the retail operations, which had been a profit generator. The period from 1926 through 1929 had been solid growth, far more successful than the manufacturing side of the business. The figures show net profit for all yards, before depletion, depreciation, interest and federal taxes. (8)

1926	1927	1928	1929	1930	1931	1932 (6 mo.)
$660k	$481k	$631k	$376k	$14k	($141k)	($ 95k)

With the national depression the number of yards dropped to 74, by the mid 30's with 20 yards closed or abandoned. A major drag on company and retail yard indebtedness was foreclosed property by the retail chain, used as collateral in selling lumber products. Fifty six dwellings, five apartments, one planer mill, one farm and a sash and door plant were foreclosed by the company during this period up to July 1932, at a value of $ 291, 493.33. (9)

A recapitulation of sales from 1935 through 1943 is listed in the Long-Bell 1943 annual report, comparing wholesale sales versus retail yard sales, illustrates the role retail yards played during this very stressful period of time.(10)

	Wholesale	Retail Yards	Total Sales	Pct Retail Yards
1935	$9.146 Mil.	$3.644 Mil.	$12.790 Mil	28%
1936	$13.648 "	$4.763 "	$18.411 "	26%
1937	$15.528 "	$5.377 "	$20.905 "	26%
1938	$12.629 "	$5.223 "	$17.852 "	29%
1939	$16.085 "	$5.224 "	$21.309 "	25%
1940	$21.979 "	$5.558 "	$27.537 "	20%
1941	$30.379 "	$7.132 "	$37.511 "	19%
1942	$35.942 "	$7.840 "	$43.782 "	18%
1943	$28.186 "	$8.779 "	$36.965 "	24%

It should be noted in these statistics, that 1938 was the worst year in the recovery from the depression and 1942/1943 show the distinct effect of World War II defense purchasing and price controls. Retail yard sales recorded $32.889 million in 1954 and $ 34.883 million in 1955.

In all of the information available, Long-Bell seemed to look favorably on educating its work force toward ideas promoting lumber products and services that fit the retail trade. Throughout the 20th century, sales meetings were held to exchange ideas, trade promotions for Long-Bell products. Guidelines for retail yard management, personal conduct of yard managers, all were constantly stressed to improve the position of Long-Bell retail yards. Exchange of ideas on how to sell specific products was always prominent on the schedule. Successful yard managers were promoted to bigger facilities or to other better jobs. Long-Bell was a great believer in promoting from within.

The Long-Bell retail lumber yard, Longview, Washington

Long-Bell had an interest in developing a retail yard system in the Western States; but due to fewer rail lines developing new territories, the company limited most of their presence to Western Washington and the Willamette Valley of Oregon. The company did have a presence in Klamath Falls, Oregon, from 1906, when the Weed Lumber Company purchased the site. Washington had 7 or 8 yards and Oregon would have up to 5 yards.

With a well managed company comes forward thinking ideas. Long-Bell moved into trade marking the lumber produced in the late teens and moved into product merchandising at the same time. Promoting their products in this manner tied the customer closer to Long-Bell as the major supplier. The retail yards developed a close relationship with their customers, providing house building plans and other promotions designed to increase the sale of lumber products. Utilizing the flow of windows, sash and doors from Weed and the Ft Smith window glazing plant enabled Long-Bell to maintain a dominant position in the market.

At the end of World War II, with the strong demand for lumber products, retail yards slowly changed to distribution facilities in larger markets and yards were sold or closed in the smaller markets. Facilities were bigger and carried a much wider range of products, more similar to what we know as Home Depot, Lowe's, etc. By 1950, there were 111 retail yards, 5 distribution facilities, 5 concrete plants, 1 prefabrication plant, and a mobile home plant, all reflecting the need for new and more diversified markets. As of the 1960's, the retail division had been reduced to 39 retail yards 5 distribution warehouses and 3 assembly plants.(11) By 1975,International Paper had closed most all of the retail yards and converted others to distribution centers. Twenty two building centers were operating across the middle west and southwest and southern portions of the country.

References:

(1)   From Tree To Trade in Yellow Pine American Lumberman July 2, 1904 Page 103

(2)   From Tree To Trade in Yellow Pine American Lumberman June 17, 1905 Page 35

(3)   From Tree To Trade in Yellow Pine American Lumberman July 2, 1904 Page 103

(4)   A great Business Organization American Lumberman April 21, 1900   Page 27

(5)   From Tree To Trade in Yellow Pine   American Lumberman Jul2, 1904 Page48&50

(6)   West Coast Lumberman Journal December 1911 Page 167

(7)   Cronwall Report Page   69

(8)   Cronwall Report Page   69

(9)   Cronwall Report Page   69

(10)   Long-Bell Annual Statement December 31, 1948

(11)   The Log Centennial Issue October/ November 1975 Page 31

THE SOUTH

Park-like terrain in Longleaf yellow pine country near DeRidder, Louisiana.

Chapter 3

SOUTHERN REGION

With the success of the Retail Yard system in the late 1880's, the company needed to find a low cost dependable supply of lumber. Initial supply sources were office wholesale outlets, with mill contacts; but it soon became apparent that this method was too costly. It was evident that the Lowe'st cost supply base was through direct contact with mills close to the retail yards. By the early 1880's investments were made with producers in Western Arkansas and Northern Louisiana for a dependable supply of lumber products. In 1889, Long-Bell purchased Barnes Lumber Company who had operations in Van Buren, Drake and Pea Ridge, Arkansas. The mill at Van Buren, Arkansas was a planning mill that bought lumber from surrounding mills within 100 miles. The other two locations were equipped with saw mills and cut both Pine and Hardwoods. (1)

The company continued to grow with the construction of a mill at Antlers, Indian Territory in 1890 and a stock purchase of controlling interest in Rapides Lumber Company, Woodworth, Louisiana in 1896. (2) In 1898 The King Ryder Lumber Company was formed to purchase a planer mill at Thomasville, Indian Territory with R. A. Long, W. S. King, W. F. Ryder and C. D. Morris as principals.

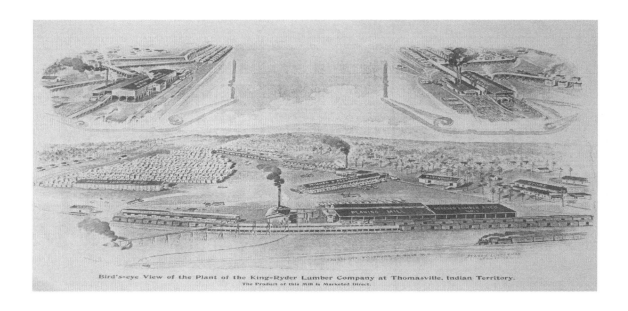

Bird's-eye View of the Plant of the King-Ryder Lumber Company at Thomasville, Indian Territory.
The Product of this Mill is Marketed Direct.

The Planer mill was purchased from Thomas Brothers who had previously operated the facility. Long-Bell secured large blocks of timber in Western Arkansas, south Of Mena, Arkansas and contracted with James L. McCoy Horatio, Arkansas (47 miles north of Texarkana, Arkansas) cutting 50,000 board feet of lumber a day to supply the mill at Thomasville, Indian Territory. (3) James L. Mc COY would build six other sawmills at Gilmore and Gravis, Arkansas, with the production being sent to the Thomasville mill, which would ship about twenty car loads per day of finished lumber. Annual production was approximately 30 million board feet with Long-Bell taking the entire production.

Sales and financial agreements had been reached with Malvern Lumber Company, Perla, Arkansas for 50% of its production. Agreements were also reached with Klondike Lumber Company, Winthrop, Arkansas, Whited and Wheless, Alden Bridge, Louisiana and R. L. Trigg Lumber Company, Noble, Louisiana for 100% of the three mills production. Long-Bell was financially involved in all three mill operations. Long-Bell advertising in "The American Lumberman Journal" of 1900 lists these mills as company production.

Long-Bell continued their pursuit of additional production, purchasing in 1898, 15,000 acres of timberland in the Hudson, Arkansas area, building a mill with a capacity of 20 million board feet, incorporating as The Hudson River Lumber Company with the mill operating until 1902. (4) Another mill, The Globe Lumber Company, Yellow Pine, Louisiana, was purchased in 1898 with 40,000 acres of timber and production capacity of 45 million board feet per year.(5)

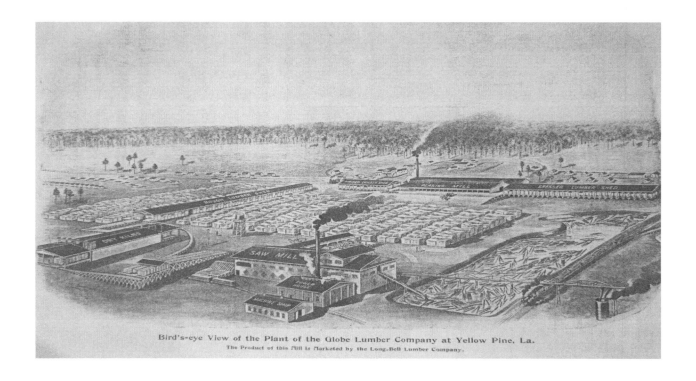

Bird's-eye View of the Plant of the Globe Lumber Company at Yellow Pine, La.
The Product of this Mill is Marketed by the Long-Bell Lumber Company.

The early 1900's saw a rapid increase in production with King- Ryder Lumber Company building a mill at Bon Ami, Louisiana with a capacity of 60 million board feet of production and 44, 000 acres of timberland. In 1902 Hudson River Lumber Company closed their mill at Hudson, Arkansas and built a new mill at De Ridder, Louisiana with a capacity of 40 million board feet and 52,000 acres to support the operation, the mill ran until 1927. (6) At that time the mill was converted to a Hardwood flooring facility, purchasing rough oak flooring strips from mills within 150 mile radius of DeRidder, Louisiana. The mill dried and surfaced the purchased product into oak flooring. In 1952 Long-Bell built a new sawmill near the site of the old mill, employing 25 men, cutting both pine and oak lumber. The Pine lumber was being cut to supply the treating plant and the oak to flooring. Oak flooring was a very important product for Long-Bell (7)

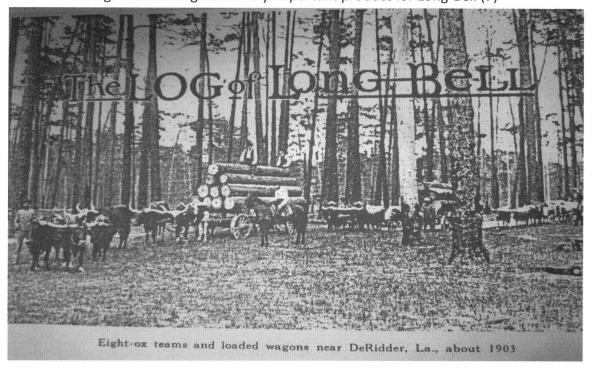

Eight-ox teams and loaded wagons near DeRidder, La., about 1903

By 1900 Long-Bell and its affiliated companies were producing 135 million board feet of lumber a year, plus purchasing an additional 40 million board feet from mills under contract and purchasing offices in Texarkana, Arkansas, Hattiesburg, Mississippi and Tacoma, Washington.

Long-Bell management was not satisfied with the status quo and continued to acquire additional mill properties and investigating others. Growth continued with the construction of a mill at Longville, Louisiana in 1907, with a capacity of 80 million board feet and operated until 1923, when the mill was destroyed by fire. The plant site was converted to oak flooring production and operated until 1926, when production was moved to the De Ridder oak flooring plant. In 1906, Long-Bell purchased the controlling interest of The Bradley- Ramsey Lumber Company, Lake

Charles, Louisiana, having invested originally in the late 1890's. They had operated two mills, Lake Charles and Mt. Holly which had a capacity of 50 million board feet and was a prime producer of export timbers, located close to ocean shipping. (8) The two mills were located adjacent to each other. Mt. Holly cut mostly for the export market until 1908 when it was converted to a picket mill. (9) It closed by 1910. The mill property was incorporated as Calcasieu Lumber Company.

Operations expanded to Arkansas, with the purchase of The Sawyer Austin Lumber Company, Pine Bluff Arkansas in 1911, forming The Arkansas Short Leaf Lumber Company which included a large tract of timber. The mill had a capacity of approximately 40 million board feet and operated until 1922 when it was destroyed by fire. In 1913 Long-Bell built a hardwood sawmill on the plant site cutting a variety of hardwood specie. In February 1917 Long-Bell signed an agreement with The Chicago Land and Timber Company for cutting rights on 125 to 130 million board feet of Hardwood timber in the Pine Bluff area, extending the life of the plant until 1928. In 1923 an additional purchase of hardwood timber was made with the acquisition of 21,684 acres from Massey-Harris Company of Toronto, Canada. (10)

Hardwoods were a very important segment of Long-Bell production as hardwood timber was interspersed with pine and flourished in river and creek bottoms. The specie that Long-Bell manufactured covered a wide range including Gum, Tupelo Gum, Red and White Oak, Beech, Ash, Basswood, Magnolia, Maple, Elm, Hickory, Cherry, Sycamore and Cottonwood. Hardwood was manufactured at all of Long-Bell mills, although over time a few locations concentrated their production toward hardwoods, especially oak flooring. In the 1920's Long-Bell was the second largest producer of Hardwoods in the United States. Long-Bell hardwood production during the period 1926 through 1931 was, 1926, 109.5 million, 1927, 101.5 million, 1928, 112 million, 1929, 87.9 million, 1930, 61 million and 1931, 46.3 million.

Markets for hardwoods were varied with the automobile market a major outlet prior to 1931. Pine Bluff was producing 50,000 spoke billets weekly for the automobile market. Truck and automobile bodies were made of hardwood. Other end uses were handles, furniture, ladders, interior trim for houses, store fixtures, phonographs, organs, picture frames, silos, toys, trunks, wagon wheels, washing machines and many other uses.

R. A. Long and his group of investors moved into the vast East Texas timberlands in 1905, forming The Lufkin Land and Timber Company, Lufkin, Texas. They purchased an established mill, with a capacity of 70 million board feet per year. The mill operated until 1930 (10). In 1911, Long-Bell had an opportunity to purchase a block of stock in Thompson-Tucker Lumber Company of East Texas, owners of 1,628,000 acres of prime East Texas timber. They were also staunch competitors of Long-Bell. Thompson- Tucker operated mills at Doucette, Trinity, Greyburg, Quincy and

Airplane view of the Long-Bell manufacturing plants at Pine Bluff, Ark.

New Willard, Texas. The stock offered was owned by an employee of Thompson- Tucker, who needed cash to pay off a debt to his employer. Had he attempted to sell it back to Thompson-Tucker, the value would have been substantially discounted. The outcome is unclear as to the stock sale; but Long-Bell and Thompson- Tucker entered into a protracted dispute which resulted in Long-Bell gaining control of Doucette, Quincy and New Willard mills in 1911. R. A. Long spoke of visiting these mills at a Board of Directors meeting December27, 1911. (11) Long-Bell advertising indicated that all four mills including Trinity were mills that Long-Bell sold product from. The Doucette mill had a capacity of approximately 35 million board feet and operated until 1945. The Quincy and New Willard mills operated for only a year or two and Trinity was dropped out as a result of the settlement of the dispute between the two companies.

In 1913 a mill and approximately 62,000 acres of timberland was acquired at Ludington, Louisiana with a capacity of 40 million board feet. The property was purchased from Ludington, Wells and Van Schaick Lumber Company. The owners originally operated in Michigan. The mill built in 1903 cut approximately 135,000 board feet per day and had the latest equipment available, including two double cut band saws and a 48" gang saw. There was only one other mill in the south with two double cut band saws. The central Louisiana mills, Ludington, Bon Ami and Longville were within four or five miles of De Ridder, Louisiana. As Long-Bell constructed these new mills, the very best equipment was installed to maximize production. Bon Ami had two single cut band saws and a large gang saw. All mills were equipped with dry kilns which could dry 100 to 150,000 board feet a day. Kiln drying was pointed toward clears as all mills had extensive stacking yards to dry dimension. Planer mills had 13 to 20 planers, sizers and matchers to process the lumber. Shipping facilities could load 15 to 25 cars a day depending on mill cut.   In 1917 a mill was acquired at Quitman, Mississippi, south of Meridian, Mississippi with a capacity of 60 to70 million board feet cutting both pine and hardwoods.(12) Quitman operated until 1932 when production was switched to Crandall, Mississippi, until the mill was destroyed by fire in 1942. Production was moved back to Quitman and ran continuously until the mill was sold in 1963. In 1952 a separate Oak flooring plant was added with volume from the Quitman mill being augmented with purchases from local mills. In the early 1920's a hardwood mill at Wilmot, Arkansas was purchased along with timberlands and operated until 1924.

Long-Bell built state of the art sawmills throughout the South and when purchasing a property, quickly brought it up to current industry standards. All of the mills had dry kilns from the early 1900's forward; however the standard method of drying lumber was by stacking in air dried yards. The kilns were used for high value clears or special items. Band saws were a new feature, reducing saw kerf significantly and developing uniform production. Labor saving devices were not a popular item at the time as labor cost was very low.

By 1915 Long-Bell and affiliated companies were producing 500 million board feet of lumber products a year from the southern mills. They continually weighed opportunities for expansion. In 1915, an opportunity to purchase 17,000 acres of timberland adjacent to the Woodworth, Louisiana mill was made available. The Gould property was eventually purchased. (13) Also cutting rights for timber owned by the Southern Pacific Railroad were negotiated; but after negotiating for several years, the railroad considered the proposal dead. This would have extended the life of the Woodward plant by several years. In East Texas efforts to acquire additional timber for the Doucette mill were successful with the acquisition of 11,000 acres from the Keith Timber interests and 15,000 acres from Kirby Timber of Texas. Efforts to acquire mill properties at Merryville, and Peason, Louisiana were not successful mainly due to lack of timber or other reasons.

Long-Bell would continue cutting hardwood lumber; but the emphasis was on oak flooring. In 1925 Long-Bell purchased Superior Oak Flooring Company, Helena, Arkansas, a plant which had five flooring machines. It would boost the production of oak flooring to its highest level. (14) The mill would run until the depression curtailed most of the south. Long-Bell added one more mill in the south with the purchase of a mill at Sheridan, Arkansas in 1944. The mill had been cutting Long-Bell timber which had been acquired in 1910 with the purchase of the Pine Bluff mill. The mill was small, cutting only about 8 million board feet per year, 80% is pine and 20% being oak and gum hardwood. (15)

Entrenched in every Long-Bell southern pine mill was an adjoining lath mill, which processed the outside slab of the log in order to reduce waste. In the era prior to pulp mills, lath was a special by-product. The house built in early to mid 1900's generally had a plastered interior as opposed to Gypsum dry wall in today's houses. Lath was produced as 3/8" or 5/16" thick by 2inches wide by four feet in length. Lath was also produced as snow fencing in prairie or mountain states as a deterrent for drifting snow. The slabs being salvaged from side cuts were usually knot free and were dropped to a processing facility beneath the sawmill and pulled out of the conveyer and ripped to the nominal size. Lath, were kiln dried to reduce weight for shipping. This was an important revenue generator for Long-Bell. If a mill did not produce lath, the material developing from side cuts usually went to a refuse burner.

Operating conditions in the southern producing area were often chaotic, having to contend with weather, financial crisis and poor business conditions. The time period prior to World War I, the United States operated as a very rural economy. For the sawmill operator, if the farmers crops did not produce the expected yield, there would be little lumber purchased. If an expected oil field did not develop the retail yards would sell very little. Financial panics had a devastating effect on commerce. Rated capacity was just that as sawmills could only run against expected sales of lumber products. Financing the mills depended on collecting the accounts receivables. Long-Bell Board of Director Meeting Notes indicate the concern that the directors had about market conditions, retail yard sales and collections and mill inventory buildup.

Standard operating procedure throughout the southern producing area was ten or eleven hours a day six days a week. Common labor was paid $1.40/ $1.50 per day for common labor with lumber graders, saw filers, sawyers, tallymen and mill wrights being paid from $2.00 to $5.00 per day. There is little evidence that operators cut wages in times of financial distress; but the universal method of balancing production to orders or market conditions was to curtail production or add a shift when conditions warranted. At Long-Bell mills, 50/60% of the jobs were classified as common labor. The black labor force was usually paid less than white labor, with the entire labor force equally split between black and white workers. Long-Bell would also utilize Hispanic labor at some locations; but discrimination was just as severe toward Hispanics as toward blacks. Japanese were used as track workers at a couple locations but Italian or Greek labor was preferred.

Weather was another serious factor affecting mill operations. There were few if any paved roads and extended periods of rain often caused the mill to run out of logs. Curtailment was the only option. On occasion violent weather would affect one of the mills in the form of tornadoes, severe thunderstorm and Hurricanes. The Globe mill reported that the smoke stack had blown down as result of a storm in May, 1908. The Doucette mill was seriously damaged by a hurricane,

May 1915, with Lufkin and Central Louisiana mills suffering minor damage. These severe storms also caused substantial damage to timber stands, which resulted in major shifting of logging plans in the affected areas. Another problem which plagued the industry was persistent railroad car shortages. Long-Bell company documents often refer to shortage of cars and its affect on the mill operations.

Timber harvesting in southern pine timber was less complicated than other areas of the country. Southern pine timber at maturity was two to four feet in diameter, growing in forests free of underbrush. The trees being 80 to 120 feet tall shadowed the area preventing the understory from growing and in many locations, fire either set or natural causes acted to keep the undergrowth to a minimum. In most areas terrain was very favorable to logging, with rolling hills or extended flat areas in which to operate. Southern Pine consisted of three main specie, Loblolly, Short Leaf and Long Leaf timber varieties, which grew in a band of timber approximately 100 miles in depth, from East Texas to Virginia.

When Long-Bell began the logging of southern pine, the existing method of log movement was to use oxen, horses or mules. Felling the tree was by axe and crosscut saw. In the days prior to railroads, logs were transported to the mill by log cart. A photo in the Long-Bell Log magazine shows a logging cart loaded with three logs which scaled at 3119 board feet. The smallest diameter was 31", 37" and 41" with the cart pulled by eight oxen. The picture was taken in the late 1890's. (16)

Long-Bell entered railroad logging in the 1890's it quickly spread to all operations. The logging camp at Woodworth, Louisiana was 16 miles from the mill, with three miles of spur track. Spur tracks were laid about 800 feet apart in order to minimize the distance for skidding logs to the rail cars.(17) Initially logs were skidded to the tracks using horse, mule or oxen teams using a logging cart called high wheels which lifted the front end of the log off the ground. This would cut down on damage to the timber stand. Each Long-Bell logging operation had a variety of animals, depending on the logging superintendent's preference. As an example, the De Ridder logging crew used 25 horses, 40 oxen and 25 mules.

In the early days of railroad logging the woods track was often narrow gauge, which was a lower cost method of operation. The rail used was 35/40# compared to main line rail was 60/65#. It was necessary to move spur tracks frequently and this helped keep costs down. All of company logging operations had rail lines 15/20 miles in length with added miles for spur tracks. As timber was felled and cut to length, the logs were pulled to the rail spur track for loading on rail cars. (18) Each Long-Bell mill would have 30 to 70 log cars for transporting the logs to the mill pond, using two or three locomotives for the task. Woods locomotives were usually smaller than main line engines, being 25/35 ton capacity while main line engines were in the 45 ton range.

By the early 1900's logs were being loaded on rail cars with steam loaders which could pull logs from a short distance to the railroad track, (a forerunner of steam skidders and the high lead logging of western woods). All logs were delivered to the log pond for sorting and storage. The average log pond could store approximately 2 million feet of logs. The skidder/ loader crew would usually load 225/250,000 feet of logs per day. There was usually competition between loading crews and it was reported in the Long-Bell Log April, 1920, a Bon Ami, Louisiana skidder crew set a record in the south, by loading 70 rail cars, 1115 logs which was 296,589 feet log scale in one day. The same crew also set a monthly record of 1224 rail cars, 20,116 logs for a total of 4,898,968 feet log scale during April 1920. The crew was 60/70 men, with the majority being black laborers. In 1904 Long-Bell had 19 woods locomotives, 796 horses, mules and oxen, 117.5 mile of railroad track and 272 rail cars used for log hauling.(19)

While Long-Bell managed their own logging operations, occasionally they would contract out areas which were either too far from mill locations or areas where terrain would be difficult to log. They found that it would be more cost effective, than with company logging crews. The Globe Lumber company tract of timber was the most difficult area and contracting was used rather extensively. With the advent of steam skidding, the pace of logging southern pine picked up dramatically. The skidder crew could pull in logs from up to 800 feet from the loading area; but the damage to uncut timber was substantial.

Even though Long-Bell management searched for additional timberland through purchasing the land or seeking exclusive cutting rights, the end of the southern operations was in sight by the early 1920's. The Globe operation closed in 1913, Bon Ami in 1925, Luddington in 1926, De Ridder old mill in1927, Lake Charles in 1928 and Lufkin in 1930. The Doucette mill operated until 1945 and Quitman continued until sold in 1963.

Long-Bell was a major producer of southern pine and hardwood lumber. By 1921 Long-Bell was the largest lumber company in the United States, producing approximately 800 million feet, in addition to being a major force in the wood treating category. The company maintained a much smaller role in southern operations throughout the succeeding years prior to merging with International Paper in 1956. Primarily through the actions tied to their early reforestation efforts and a climate that encouraged rapid growth the south is still a major producer of lumber, plywood and particleboard products. Timber size is much smaller, averaging 16/24" in diameter, with much of the timberlands in form of plantations, averaging 500 to 600 trees to the acre. Logging is done by use of mechanical equipment such as the Feller-Buncher. This machine has a massive set of shears to cut the tree, strip the branches and cut the log to length all in one operation. Milling equipment has been revised to meet the smaller log size. Chip-n-saws, plywood lathes handling peeler blocks down to 8" in diameter and other features to handle smaller diameter timber. While Long-Bell did not survive to see the changes, its successor company International Paper thrives today as a major forest products company.

References:

(1) Log of Long-Bell   November 1919 Page 14

(2) From Tree to Trade in Yellow Pine   American Lumberman   July 4, 1904 Pages 82 to 85

(3) A Great Business Organization   American Lumberman   April 21, 1900   Pages 36

(4) From Tree to Trade in Yellow Pine   American Lumberman   July 4, 1904   Page 89

(5) From Tree to Trade in Yellow Pine   American Lumberman   July 4, 1904 Page 91

(6) Log of Long-Bell May 1955   Pages 4 to6

(7) Log of Long-Bell   November 1952   Page 4 to 6

(8)   Robert Alexander Long   A Lumberman Of The Gilded Age Lenore K. Bradley Page 35

(9) Long-Bell Board of Directors Meeting Notes   January21, 1908 Page 2

(10) Texas Forestry Museum Texas Sawmill Data Base December 4, 1995

(11)   Long-Bell Board OF Director Meeting Notes   December27,1911

(12) Log of Long-Bell   June 1955   Page 8 to10

(13) Long-Bell Board of Director Meeting Notes   May 15, 1917

(14) Log of Long-Bell November 1925   Page3

(15) Log of Long-Bell   1955   Pages 8 to 10

(16) Log of Long-Bell November 1919 Page 14

(17) From Tree to Trade in Yellow Pine   American Lumberman   July 4, 1904 Page 88

(18) From Tree to Trade in Yellow Pine   American Lumberman   July 4, 1904 Page 88

(19) From Tree to Trade in Yellow Pine   American Lumberman   July 4, 1904 Page 116

Chapter 4

SALES AND MARKETING

With the establishment of lumber production of Southern Pine, Long-Bell soon had more volume of lumber than the existing chain of retail yards could absorb. At the time of acquiring their first sawmill, the company made a conscious decision that mill production would not be dedicated to the retail system. In 1885, ten years after the formation of Long-Bell a purchasing office was established, Sabine Valley Lumber Company, Texarkana, Arkansas. The original purpose was to supply the retail chain; but the successful venture soon developed supply capabilities allowing the company to sell the excess to the mill direct and to wholesale markets. Sabine Valley Lumber Company employed eleven personnel, with some of them being involved in selling lumber into the Southwestern markets of the United States.(1) The enterprise was managed by S. T. Woodring who had developed experience in retail yard management and wholesale sales in Kansas, Missouri and Oklahoma Indian Territory. He had been associated with C. B. Sweet, vice president and assistant General Manager of Long-Bell. The Sabine Valley Lumber Company was quite successful selling product from contract mills in Arkansas and Louisiana, often competing with mills owned by Long-Bell. As Long-Bell added mills throughout Louisiana, Texas and Arkansas, each mill would have one or two salesmen to market the product of the mill and competing with the other mills in the system as well as the wholesale function.

In 1886, a new company, Long- Mansfield was opened up in Columbus, Ohio as a wholesale office. It was later moved to St. Louis, Missouri, with traveling salesmen who sold throughout the central Midwest states as well as the southwest. (2) Business grew rapidly and a buying office was opened in Hattiesburg, Mississippi and later Lake Charles, Louisiana to supply the increased sales. It is interesting to note that the wholesale operations dealt in Southern Pine lumber, Cypress lumber and shingles, Douglas Fir lumber, Ponderosa Pine lumber and Red Cedar shingles.

The need to supply West Coast Douglas Fir lumber and Red Cedar shingles prompted Long-Bell to open a purchasing office in Tacoma, Washington in1893 which was the center of West Coast lumber production at that time and provided sources of product for purchase. W. A. Lyman was the initial manager, followed by E. R. Rogers in 1894. Red Cedar shingles were the primary roof covering of the time and Long-Bell established a concentration yard in Tacoma, Washington with an inventory of thousands of squares of shingles. Long-Bell would be one of the first companies to ship shingles and lumber unsold, selling the product as it moved across the country.

Long-Bell was very active in purchasing western lumber and shingle products, from 1893 through 1911 according to The West Coast Lumberman Journal, December 1911 issue. In announcing the closure of the Long-Bell purchasing office in 1912, it was disclosed that the company averaged 1600 carloads a year during the time it was open, with one year having purchased 2400 car loads. Long-Bell would continue western purchasing activities from Kansas City, Missouri, under the name Pacific Coast Products. In addition to purchasing western requirements, a distribution yard in Kansas City, Missouri was operated, carrying all of the species being purchased (3)

By 1897, wholesale sales operations, were incorporated within the company structure and managed by M. B. Nelson who remained in charge of sales until 1923 when he was elevated to President of The Long-Bell Lumber Company. Long-Bell established sales offices, throughout the Southwest and Central States, to move the volumes produced by their own and contract mills. By 1900 they were selling 179 million board feet of lumber through retail and wholesale outlets. (4)

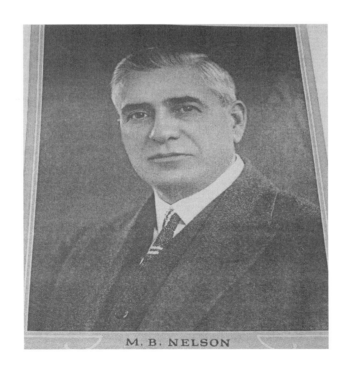

M. B. NELSON

As Long-Bell began to produce lumber in Western Louisiana, Arkansas and East Texas, the mills operated as independent companies, with one or more salesmen who traveled the Southwest and lower Middle West. As production increased, the company added salesmen who worked out of the Kansas City office. At that time in the late 1890's and early 1900's, salesmen were recruited from the mills and were well trained in the capabilities and products of the mills where they worked. As time went on, additional salesmen were hired having worked at competitor mills, or in the retail lumber trade. As the country grew, demand for lumber products prompted producers to expand their sales organization. New sales territories opened up quickly and Long-Bell was in the lead by moving into major Metropolitan markets. By 1904 the company consolidated all sales through Kansas City, Missouri, eliminating the mill salesman. Long-Bell salesmen now covered the entire portion of the country, east of the Rocky Mountains with but a few exceptions. The rapidly developing Plains states began purchasing greater volumes from Southern Pine sources as the White Pine supply from Michigan, Minnesota and Wisconsin dried up. Competition from West Coast sources was developing; but rail tariffs were high enough to allow Southern Pine ready access. By the late teens, the Long-Bell sales force had grown to 40 and handled sales of Southern Pine, Treated products, Sash and Door and Hardwoods While a majority of the salesmen concentrated on lumber sales, specialists worked the Treated and Sash and Door product lines.

Long-Bell was constantly looking for new markets for their Southern Pine production. In 1904 the company entered into the export market through the ports of Beaumont and Port Arthur, Texas and Lake Charles, Louisiana. The volume of export lumber was attractive enough to Long-Bell, that facilities were developed at Port Arthur, Texas to hold two to five million feet of timbers and two to three million feet of lumber. The port at Beaumont, Texas had a floating boom which could hold twenty million feet of lumber products. In the years prior to World War I, Long-Bell chartered vessels to carry their products to foreign markets. All lumber and timber items shipped into the export markets were branded with the Long-Bell name. (5)

Export markets required that product be shipped in metric sizes, often resulting in cutting odd sizes not used in domestic markets. The monetary gain was sufficient to warrant competing in this market. Long Lengths and high quality Clears were the preferred items and Long-Bell timber lands could provide the items needed. By 1912 Long-Bell was shipping approximately 80 million board feet a year and the company established an export department headed up by Roy Morse who had been based at Lake Charles followed by Lloyd L. Chipman, who would be associated with export until 1934, when the function was absorbed into the general sales group. With the formation of the export function, an office was opened in Hamburg, Germany. Sales were made to Germany, Great Britain, the European Continent, South Africa and elsewhere. With the limited communications capability, it is surprising how much volume was shipped offshore from the United States.

Long-Bell was noted for its capability to produce special items and having mills on or close to shipping ports was a valuable asset.

As the volume grew and the market place became more selective, changes were required by Long-Bell and other producers, in order to maintain their respective positions in the lumber market. Quality of lumber products was of great concern in the market place. The grade of lumber received varied widely, with some companies (Long-Bell included) being favorably preferred over others. It was common practice for retail yards to push a favored producer's product over another, to the point where they began to rely on the favored one exclusively. Grades product names and sizes varied from mill to mill. Customers favored mills whose quality was consistent and quality producers preferred to ship consistent grades, rather than high grading to a particular customer. Long-Bell was a preferred supplier in all markets.

Formalized grading of lumber was begun as early as 1891, when the Mississippi Valley Lumbermen's Association prepared a set of grading rules for White Pine Lumber. The rules went into effect in 1894. As early as 1901, The Pacific Coast Lumbermen's Association adopted uniform grading rules and these were adopted by other coast associations which eventually became The West Coast Lumbermen's Association. The Southern Pine Lumbermen would begin about the same time.

As early as the turn of the century, pressure was building to formulate national grading standards for common grades and sizes of lumber. From a competitive standpoint, lumber producers needed to know what other producers included in a particular grade category and sizes shipped. Long-Bell purchased large volumes of lumber from other producers and had considerable influence over grade quality and sizes. Quality had to be maintained to sustain the reputation developed throughout the Long-Bell organization. With the ever growing usage of lumber, there was a critical need for federal commercial standards among all producers, whether Southern Pine, Douglas Fir, Ponderosa Pine, Redwood or Northern Pine production. While each producer had to stand on its own reputation, there was enough difference between grades and sizes in the producing regions to warrant one standard for all.

In May 22, 1922, the Secretary of Commerce, Herbert H. Hoover called a weeklong conference in Washington D. C., inviting representatives of lumber producers, wholesalers, retail yards, large consumers and government officials. The purpose as described in the resolution:

"Resolved that all organizations, representing producers, consumers and distributors of lumber, be invited to appoint representatives to meet in general conference on the call of the National Lumber Manufacturers Association, with the assistance of the Departments of Commerce and Agriculture, for the purpose of arranging for holding meetings in as many sections of the United States as may be deemed necessary in order to arrive at definite recommendations concerning the three subjects here under discussion; such recommendations to be placed before another general conference of all interests involved after the series of sectional conferences shall have been concluded. (6) The three areas to consider at the conference were; 1) A change in nomenclature of lumber so that the same article would be known by the same name throughout the country. 2) Grade marking and means of designating to the consumer more clearly the parameters of what the grade consisted, so they can tell what they are buying. 3) Standardization of sizes of the different species. With these changes every lumber product will have its own grading rules, names and sizes.

Long-Bell executives named to prestigious committees, were J. W. Martin (quality and grade marking) and M. B. Nelson (committee on nomenclature). A third committee was established to develop a standard for claims and inspection procedures. The customer base had a serious need for simple procedures to gain satisfaction in adjudicating complaints on grade and tally.

The Secretary of Commerce urged the participants to arrive on common ground on the major areas of concern. After many meetings, drafts and changes, a commercial standard for lumber products was developed in 1924. The American softwood lumber standard, established lumber sizes, methodology for assigning design values, nomenclature, inspection and re-inspection procedures, an accreditation program and other functions to keep current with ever changing needs of consumers, regulators and manufacturers.

In 1941, The National Lumber Manufacturers Association (N.L.M.A.) entered into a consent decree with the U. S. District Court. The consent decree required the N. L. M. A. to create an impartial agency to oversee the standardization, certification and accreditation for softwood lumber. In 1953, the court found that the American Lumber Standard Committee (A.C.L.S.) appointed by the Secretary of Commerce and it's independently elected Board of Review, were impartial bodies appropriate to carry out the decree. Today the A. C. L. S. continues to operate under the consent decree and the voluntary standards system of the Department of Commerce. With its initial beginnings in 1922, the system works well in today's business climate, thanks to companies such as Long-Bell's enthusiastic support. All categories of wood products, Plywood, Treated, Laminated products and pressed board products operate using this system.

With the pending construction of the Longview mill, improved export sales would be a major factor in the success of the new mill. Using data provided by the federal Department of Commerce in 1921, Long-Bell executives looked favorably at expansion of chartering vessels or owning their own vessels carrying the company flag. Constant investigation of market potential was necessary in order to position the company toward taking full advantage of the new production. Europe had always been a market favored by Long-Bell and in 1921, Lloyd L. Chipman, Export Sales Manager was sent to survey markets in Great Britain, France, Germany, Holland and Belgium, as these countries were all recovering from the effects of World War I. Statistics from the Department of Commerce indicated that the potential was great, with individual summaries from each country. (7)

As with any product, lumber fit into specific shortages around the world. Douglas Fir, Southern Pine and Hardwood species were desirable to augment Northern Europe's dependence on Spruce and Balsam from Russia, Scandinavian and other Eastern Europe specie. In the Far East, North American products would fill the need for structural timber as the predominant specie, Mahogany was used for decorative and furniture purposes.

Dealing in export markets required considerable education as foreign practices were considerably different than domestic. In countries such as Great Britain, Holland, Belgium, Italy and Spain, large volumes of native timber were scarce. These countries would be considered net importers of product to satisfy their own domestic markets. A major use of lumber and panel products is not housing as it is in the United States. Wood product end use in European markets tended toward packaging, concrete forming and heavy construction. North Europe housing is built with concrete, stone or cement blocks and the practice continues today despite efforts by American and Canadian agencies and companies involved with export sales.

Continuing their investigation of world export opportunities in 1923, Lloyd L. Chipman and M. B. (Mike) Nelson, General Sales Manager for Long-Bell and their wives made a trip to Japan and China with the Chipmans, going on to Australia at the completion of the Orient trip. The Nelsons would be gone six months, the Chipmans for nine months. The most expeditious method travel in those days was by steamship. The Orient had been a market for West Coast products since the 1850's; but little was known about the market potential. It was a normal situation to spend three to six months or more on an overseas trip when visiting more than one country. It was indicative of Long-Bell management support of a viable export sales program to send the vice president of sales and head of the export program to the Orient in search of long term connections. With the new Longview mill on the horizon, the ability to move product in large volumes to the export market was of upmost importance. When up and running, the Longview mill would produce almost as much as the existing southern mills combined. (8)

The lumber market in Japan, where housing is primarily of wood construction was estimated to be 1.7 billion to 2.0 billion board feet in 1922. It was estimated at the time that approximately 600 million board feet would come from United States sources. Japan has always been prone to earthquakes and building codes favored wood products for homes and commercial buildings. Japan was limited in its ability to provide lumber products from native species. Imports from Russian Siberia, Mongolia, The Philippines and Dutch East India supplied the balance. Shipments from Siberia and

Mongolia were often uncertain, making the prospects from the United States more favorable. Japan was one country that practiced extensive re-forestation; but the efforts were in the beginning stage. With a growing population the Japanese appetite for forest products would only increase in the 20ᵗʰ century. (9)

The Japanese lumber industry during the 1920's was made up of many small sawmills employing very few people. The importation of "Jap Squares" from West Coast mills was the most satisfactory method to import forest products to meet the needs of the Japanese markets. Wood products exported to Japan from North American sources were divided into several categories. Logs, squared timbers 12" x12" to 36" x 36" and Cedar bolts (split Cedar sections 8' long). These products had been shipped from West Coast ports since the early 1900's. Squares imported into Japan would be purchased by small mills, one or two at a time and re-sawn to local specifications. The Japanese market situation would continue to demand sizeable quantities of lumber products up to World War II and increasing rapidly after the war.

With the opening of the Panama Canal in early teens, a new market opportunity occurred for West Coast producers as green lumber was shipped to East Coast ports of the United States. Tremendous volumes of lumber would flow from Oregon, Washington and British Columbia through the Panama Canal to ports from Florida to Massachusetts. The opening of the Canal also shortened the distance and sailing time to North Europe and Mediterranean and African locations. The new mill being built at Longview would give Long-Bell an advantage over Southern and East Coast mills. (10)

Lloyd L. Chipman and M. B. (Mike) Nelson surveyed the Chinese and Japanese markets together, finding that Japan being a much smaller country was much better organized for importing product from the West. It was surprise to Nelson and Chipman how extensive the Chinese forest land was although the industry was extremely disorganized during the time of their trip. It was evident from this tour that they had developed a good understanding of the flow of lumber products throughout this section of the world and how Long-Bell could be a major participant. (11)

Lloyd Chipman went on to study markets in Australia and New Zealand as part of the exploration for export opportunities. His reception was highly favorable and possibilities for Douglas Fir and Hemlock were good, with Hemlock the favored specie throughout the 20ᵗʰ century. 6"x12" and wider was the prominent size, due to import duty restrictions. It is almost impossible to import smaller sized material due to competitive local factors for native timber.

With the completion of the West mill in 1924, export became a critical outlet for production. Size of raw material was so much larger than ever previously considered that the mill could take on large items with ease. As a result of the exploratory trip by Chipman and Nelson, Long-Bell quickly secured orders for 36"x36" 80 feet long which few mills could produce. The export market required special cuttings in almost every inquiry. It was a requirement at every export mill that a special cutting list was posted by the head sawyer. Sizes such as 2"x10" 40 foot #2 clear vertical grain, or 4"x12" #1 rough or 10"x10" #1 common 70 feet long were all considered special cutting. To produce some of these items, logs were selected in the woods and identified when delivered to the mill. The West Fir mill at Longview was one of the few mills in the west that could cut anything from a 4"x4" to 36"x36" up to 80 feet long. Long-Bell was selected to cut 34"x34" #1 common 80 feet long, for the Panama Canal in the mid 1920's. In the period prior to and following World War II Long-Bell produced ship decking for aircraft carriers and other naval vessels. Douglas Fir ship decking was usually 6/4" x4" and 6/4" x 6" # 2 vertical grain clear up to 60 feet long. During World War II, the majority of the entire mill production was shipped over the cargo docks as the military and Russian aid took precedence over all other shipments.

Long-Bell served as a leader in many of the modern aspects of business through the forward thinking of its managers. Long-Bell service and quality was a top priority for the company. The objective of the company was to develop repeat business from the customer base was paramount to its success. Quality and service was stressed throughout the organization, with repeated examples of performance featured in "The Long-Bell Log". Many examples of customers requesting quick shipment of an order were rewarded with a wire to the mill and a railroad car number sent back in the next day or two. The company stressed throughout the organization, the need to strive to be the best in the industry. Complaints about service or quality, while few, were addressed quickly. The company continually advertised customer favorable comments. The sales force and mill personnel were considered as part of a team, with both organizations made familiar with each other's role. (12)

As Long-Bell expanded its sales force into most areas of the United States, it recognized that more needed to be done to put the company name in front of the customer on a sustained basis. The company was very proud of the products it produced as to quality and acceptance by the customer. In June 1919 the company announced that it would begin to stamp the Long-Bell name on every piece of lumber produced. Placing the company name on the end of each piece would prove to be a great advertisement for the organization. Long-Bell had a long experience with trade marking as every piece of export lumber had the company name on the end of the piece since 1904.(13) Other companies would follow Long-Bell's lead. Weyerhaeuser began trade marking all of its lumber in 1928, although they had tried doing it in the early 1920's and the Idaho mills stamped Genuine White Pine beginning in 1924. The investment soon began to show results as customers were enthusiastic about promoting Long-Bell production as the best. (14)

Coupled with quality, service and end branding, came a corporate advertising policy. Local retail yards and individual mills had used various methods of advertising, to alert the trade to the benefits of using Long-Bell products. In 1919, the company began an extensive advertising campaign, designed to expand the company sales penetration throughout the country. The Long-Bell advertising campaign was estimated to have reached 212 million readers. These advertisements were distributed to a wide range of   publications, about half to national publications such as Saturday Evening Post and Literary Digest and the balance to trade publications. (15)

By the 1920's Long-Bell was one of the largest lumber companies in the United States, with offices in most major cities, plus a strong Export sales program. Management was generous in making sure they had the best trained sales force in the business. Sales meetings, mill trips and promotion from within, were aimed at gaining the maximum effort from the salesmen. Salesmen were viewed by the customer as being" Long-Bell", representing the company in all aspects of business. The salesman was urged to provide any service to the customer. (16)

Sales management continually stressed the importance of teamwork. Viewing the company as a team, where sales, advertising and manufacturing had to operate in complete cooperation, as the failure of one segment was a failure for all. The sales message continually pointed toward quality and service, with the objective of being the key supplier to the customer. Retail customers were becoming more sophisticated with improved communications and demanded consistent quality and service. (17)

Long-Bell was known to be somewhat higher in price than the average producer. Quality and service coupled with the advertising program were cited as reasons for maintaining this posture. Management placed the burden of selling this philosophy on the salesman, with the strong argument that quality and service would be a major benefit to the customer. Depending on the market situation, Long-Bell would act to guarantee prices for a month at a time. This would occur in strong markets when there seemed to be a flurry of buying. (18) Coupled with this firm price, was a strict policy limiting sales volume to that which could be shipped in 30 days. This practice was designed to maintain a stable market place and allow the customer the ability to quote to his customer with confidence that goods would be delivered knowing that the price had not moved up in the meantime. At other times the company would restrict the salesmen from soliciting orders, as the price would be too low. (19)

Long-Bell believed in educating their sales force and supporting them with updated mill information, through mill visits and sales meetings. These were held where mill, sales and management personnel would come together to discuss the current situation, problems or new opportunities. On an annual basis in the late teens and early 1920's, the entire sales force would meet, generally the last week of the year, at Kansas City, MO., for a review of the company situation. The gathering would encompass up to 100 personnel from every segment of the company. R. A. Long would usually address the group, along with informative presentations by key manufacturing, sales, credit, traffic and advertising management.

Plans for the next year advertising expenditures would be carefully outlined, as this had an impact on the individual salesman's territory. New products would be explained in detail and reviews of sales and credit policy were thoroughly discussed. One of the highlights of the sessions was the selection of a salesman to discuss success stories in selling lumber products. Subjects such as Competition Teamwork and Sales (Treated 1924), Selling Miscellaneous and Short Lengths (1919 and 1924), How I Increased Hardwood Sales 800% and Modern Selling Methods were indicative of the detail some of the successful salesmen approached their jobs. Another highlight would be the selection of a key customer to address the group on successful salesmanship, trade marking, customer service and advertisement benefits. These discussions had a definite effect on the sales force, as they could see positive results form company policies. An added benefit was the presentation would show up in the Long-Bell Log in subsequent publications reinforcing the message. (20)

Long-Bell Cedar Shingle Concentration Yard
circa Early 1900's
Sixteenth and California Street, Tacoma, Washington

As Long-Bell continued to increase its volume of product to sell, the recruitment of sales personnel shifted from mill to the college campus. While the occasional salesman was selected from mill ranks, the increased need, forced the company to look elsewhere for the skilled sales force. Sales trainees were selected from colleges and universities, often a Forestry school. A trainee would spend from one to two years at the mill level, working primarily in the planer and shipping departments with skilled lumber graders and others to learn the lumber business from the ground up. Mill management would discuss all factors involved in operating the business, so they would have complete exposure prior to moving out to a sales territory. From the mill exposure, time would be spent in the central office in Kansas City, moving from one desk to another to gain the knowledge needed to operate a territory. The sales trainee program started sometime in the late Teens and continued well into the 1950's and early 1960's after Long-Bell merged with International Paper. The training program also served to supply the industry with well experienced employees as Long-Bell employees moved on to other opportunities.

Four ocean freighters loading lumber at the Long-Bell docks. Longview, Wn.

Long-Bell Log May 1928

The sales force grew from 25/30 in the early 1900's, 45/50 in the 1920's, 75/80 in the 1930's /1940's to 140 in 1965 which included 21 distribution centers. As the Long-Bell Division was integrated further into International Paper, production was on the decline, product lines began to be more specialized and the role of the road salesman was in decline. With Long-Bell's presence in the market place, the long time service of its sales force and the progressive policies of the company, it certainly ranked as one of the best in the business.

References:

(1)   A Great Business Organization, American Lumberman, April 21, 1900, Page   32

(2)   A Great Business Organization, American Lumberman April 21, 1900, Page   30

(3)   West Coast Lumberman Journal, December 1911, Page 167

(4)   Long-Bell Log, August 1923, Page 6

(5)   Long-Bell Log, February 1922, Page 5

(6)   Long-Bell Log, June 1922, Page 2 to 5

(7)   Long-Bell Log, June 1921, Page 10/11

(8)   Long-Bell Log, February 1923, Page   12

(9)   Long-Bell Log, June 1923, Page 2

(10)   Long-Bell Log, February 1923, Page 10/11

(11)   Long-Bell Log, June 1923, Page 2 to 5

(12)   Long-Bell Log, September 1925, Page 8

(13)   Long-Bell Log, April 1924,   Page 17

(14)   Timber and Men Hildy Hill and Neven, Page 366 to 368

(15)   Long-Bell Log, January 1919, Page 6

(16)   Long-Bell Log, July 1922, Page 6

(17)   Long-Bell Log, January 1923, Page 6

(18)   Long-Bell Log, September 1919, Page 10/11

(19)   West Coast Lumberman Journal, January 1909, Pages 236/237

(20)   Long-Bell Log, March 1924, Page 10

Chapter 5

TREATED PRODUCTS

One of the most important product categories Long-Bell was involved in was Treated products. In 1916 the company opened a Creosote treating facility at Shreveport, Louisiana to service a growing need for a product designed to withstand the pervasive soil and water conditions of the South. Principal products were Paving Blocks, Fence Posts and Piling. Telephone Poles and Railroad Ties would be added to service the growing rail line expansion and the rapid use of electricity. By 1917 a facility was added at De Ridder, Louisiana and in 1919 a facility was opened at Marion, Illinois. The three plants were operated by American Treating Company with Long-Bell supplying the raw material and selling the finished product.(1)

By 1922, there were 122 treating facilities in the United States, mainly in the South. Eighty nine of these plants were commercial facilities selling on the open market, while others were operated by Railroads and Electrical companies to treat their own products. From the inception in the mid teens, to 1922, the majority of product moved throughout the south; but by 1924 treated products began to move across the entire country.

The Long-Bell treating plants were supplied from company timber holdings and outside timber operators for posts, poles and piling with sawn railroad ties produced at company mills and also local mills specializing in tie manufacture. Long-Bell found that in stands of Southern Pine and cutover land, there were large quantities of small timber, not suited for saw logs but ideal for serving the treated market. These trees were of sufficient size and straightness to make quality posts and poles. Timber tracts in the late 1890's and under the control of Long-Bell were located close to the Shreveport and De Ridder treating plants. The Bowman tract of timber, located in Sabine Parish, Louisiana consisted of 21,160 acres of cut over land and the Trigg tract, Noble, Sabine Parish, Louisiana, consisted of 18,920 acres, both being very close to the Shreveport facility. Long-Bell had financed the saw mills that had made the first cutting. (2)

The contract with the American Treating Company, called for Long-Bell to supply 20 million feet of posts, telephone poles, railroad ties and other material to be treated at the Shreveport facility. The contract called for a penalty for treating less than 20 million feet and a bonus for treating over 25 million feet. Long-Bell had the right to purchase the De Ridder facility after operating for two and one half years. (3) In 1928 the company opened a treating facility in Kansas City, Missouri. The Sheridan, Arkansas forest reserve, consisting of 77,245 acres would supply the raw material. This forest sold to other treating plants in the vicinity as well as to local sawmills.

The telephone poles were taken from the forest ahead of commercial logging. The poles were cut from 20 to 55 foot lengths, depending on the order specifications. Posts were cut to length, 6 and 8 foot in length and sorted into seven groups. Longer posts were often ripped to half or quartered to make another grade of post. The treating plant operated retorts 7 feet in diameter and 40 feet long. The treatment under pressure was with Creosote Oil.

Long-Bell Log - Longview Treating Plant

With increased interest in reforestation, thinning planted acres were an ideal source for the fence post market. During the early 1920's, forestry clubs were created at local high schools throughout Louisiana. The club's were sponsored by the Louisiana State Division of Forestry and were designed to interest boys in reforestation and to provide considerable timber for commercial purposes. It was also used to educate the older generation on the long term, benefits of timber regeneration. The forestry clubs were encouraged to develop plots from one to three acres. In the first year, 1000 plots were formed, with fire protection and thinning of key importance. Competitions were held in each parish (county) and a prize given for the best ones. (4) The development of this program required an outlet for the posts and poles developed. Long-Bell was in the forefront and quickly signed on as a purchaser of product and supporter of the program. Logs, ties (hand hewed and sawn), fence posts, telephone poles and piling were products purchased by Shreveport, and De Ridder, Louisiana treating plants. In addition pulpwood was another byproduct from these plots, taking wood down to a three inch, diameter. As the market for treated products grew, lumber products were added to the product line. Railroad ties were a major item as the nations railroad system continued to expand. Bridge timbers were also added to the mix of items.

Selling treated products proved difficult in the early days, primarily due to cost. The southern climate was quite detrimental to wood products, due to the high temperatures and moist conditions, causing the wood to deteriorate quickly. Treated products proved to be more stable than untreated but cost about 40% more. In order to be successful in selling treated, it became very apparent that the end use customer needed to be convinced of the benefits. Tests showing that treated items had a lifetime four to five times longer than untreated, soon convinced customers to use the treated product.

In 1918, the treated division shipped 1,400,000 posts distributed through 1200 retail yards, furnished poles for 1000 miles of railway right of way and many miles of electrical transmission lines. In 1919, Long-Bell was prepared to ship 3 ½ million posts. (5) In order to increase the market penetration of treated products, it was necessary to include special services for some products. All of the posts, poles and piling were debarked prior to treating. Telephone poles were bored and framed prior to treatment, based on specifications supplied by the customer.

Treating plants were very labor intensive, as debarking was done by hand. The Shreveport plant employed as many as 300 men to handle the product moving through the treating retorts. Over the years, improvements in equipment would significantly reduce the number of employees needed to operate the plants. In addition to high employment, the need to carry large inventories of product line tied up significant capital. Shreveport had an inventory space for one million posts and De Ridder had space for 750 thousand posts, in addition to the need for inventory of piling, poles, ties and other items, both treated and untreated.(6)

Treated demand continued to grow and Long-Bell would expand production and sales on a regular basis. In 1937 the Shreveport, Louisiana facility was closed and equipment transferred to Joplin, Missouri. The Marion, Illinois plant was closed in 1929 and De Ridder doubled in size. Also in 1937, Long-Bell opened a treating facility at Weed, California. The facility was built and operated by American Treating under contract to Long-Bell, with the company furnishing the raw material and sales representation.(7) By 1945, another treating cylinder was added at DeRidder and in 1947, a treating facility was added at Longview, Washington and in 1955, a facility was acquired at Navasota, Texas (close to College Station, Texas) to serve the Houston and South Texas market.

Posts produced from thinning longleaf pine

Long-Bell Log June 1927

The Southern and Middle West facilities were oriented toward fence posts, poles and railroad ties in the early years, with lumber products being added as demand grew. The Weed facility had a capacity of 15 million feet per year, treated primarily poles, piling lumber, railroad ties and some posts and plywood in later years. All of the plants were creosote oil; but Weed and Longview offered Wolman Salts treatment after the 1950's. Wolman Salt treatment was used for Plywood, Gutter and Framing Lumber. Longview and Weed had the capacity to treat up to 120 feet in length for poles, piling and Laminated products.

As Long-Bell's second growth forests in the West developed, a prime source of raw material for the Longview plant emerged. Forest stands of 45/80 years of age were thinned generating large quantities of telephone poles and piling. The market for posts was not as important as at the Southern plants. Piling required long straight timber up to 120 feet long and 20/36" butt diameter. The trees selected for piling were felled and debarked on a special order basis. Although the Longview plant was supplied on special orders from the Ryderwood Tree Farm, their major supply came from local timber suppliers.

The treating plants operated as independent facilities, purchasing their raw material from local timber suppliers, as well as company sources. DeRidder brought raw material from a 150 mile radius to the plant. The Joplin, Missouri plant had two satellite post operations at Licking and Raymondville, Missouri utilizing private lands on a contract basis and some product from southeast Missouri national forests. In addition, 36,000 acres of company timber holdings in western and central Arkansas supplied posts and poles to Joplin, Missouri. Areas of company holdings in Louisiana and east Texas provide posts and poles to De Ridder and the Navasota, Texas plants.

The treating division was a key contributor to company profits from its inception. Company profit statements are difficult to locate, and treated products were not reported separately. The years prior to the depression illustrate the favorable position treated products had in the corporate structure. The years 1926 through the first six months of 1932, illustrate the strong position of the treated product line.

Net Profit

1926	1927	1928	1929	1930	1931	1932 (6 months)
$285.4	$276.2	$211.5	$295.5	$116.6	$184.4	$32.5

Percent Earned on Investment

31.6%	25.3%	18.6%	25.0%	10.3%	22.6%	4.1%

The treated plants remained an important segment of the Long-Bell organization; but with the absorption of the Long-Bell Division into International Paper, closures began to occur. The Weed plant closed in 1975, although the facility continues to operate as J. H. Baxter Inc. The other facilities continued to operate until mid to late 1980's with the exception of Longview which closed in 1981, with balance continuing until the mid to late 80's.

One factor not considered in the development of treated facilities, was the cleanup required as plants closed. With the impact of the environmental movement in the 70's and refinements in later years, the cost of removing tainted soil and chemicals was substantial. Treated lumber continues to be a significant segment of the wood products industry.

We, the employees of the Joplin, Mo., Wood Preserving Division, are proud to be members of the Long-Bell Family, doing our part in creating products that bear the TRADE MARK OF QUALITY. —Joplin Long-Bell Employees

Left to right: (1) R. C. Starling and J. D. Hughes, track maintenance, keep the yard tracks in repair. (2) Otto Boyd and Lieutenant Burton load posts for rail shipment. (3) Charles Daves and Emmett Foy hook a sling of poles. (4) Calvin Bates, head framer, and framers Everett Poe, Lewis Robertson, Norman Griffin, and Basil Sparlin frame poles in the yard. (5) Top loaders Esaw Edwards and Walter Fields stack poles. (6) The pole machine trims knots and surface irregularities even with the body of the pole or piling. Oville Bates, pole machine helper in the foreground; Harry Vicory, checker; Everett Poe, framer; and Frank Daugherty, helper.

Long-Bell Log October 1957 Joplin Treating

References:

(1) Long-Bell Log, October , 1959, Page 8

(2) Cronwall Report, Page 62

(3) Cronwall Report, Page 115

(4) Long-Bell Log , February 1926, Page 7/8

(5) Long-Bell Log, December 1919, Page 12/13

(6) Long-Bell Log, December 1919, Page 12/13

(7) Long-Bell Log, October 1959, Page 8

Chapter 6

OTHER OPPORTUNITIES

In the normal course of business, opportunities outside of usual operations were present-ed to Long-Bell management and the Board of Directors, which warranted investigation and often action. Some of the areas of interest were related to the core business, such as Naval Stores and Cutover Land Sales, while other opportunities such as Gas and Oil came as a result of attempting to gain value from cutover land. Ventures such as Coal and Wooden Ship building presented an opportunity that had appeal at the time of decision. Some were successful, while others were not.

With the expansion of the retail yard system and growth in lumber production, it seemed to be a natural fit to experiment with other product opportunities. Coal was one of those prod-ucts, which fit the retail system and was plentiful in Missouri, Kansas and Arkansas. It was the standard fuel for homes and business establishments and it was a major item for sale in retail yards. In 1898, Long-Bell formed The Fidelity Land and Investment Company and The Fidelity Fuel Company to develop coal properties in Cherokee and Crawford Counties, Kansas and early in 1900 a mine at Fidelity, Arkansas was opened. (1) In 1900, mining also began at Stone City, Kan-sas, with five mines in operation by 1903, with a potential of six million tons of semi-anthracite coal. In 1903 a sales department was formed, headed by L. L. Chipman to move the product of the mines. In 1903 the mines initially proved profitable with total sales of 21, 500,000 pounds of coal. Beginning in 1907, problems began to occur, with numerous comments about rail car shortages. The mine properties operated at approximately 50%of capacity, which related to the car supply problem. (2) This occurred despite the fact that a major percentage of coal sales were to the Frisco, Rock Island and Southern Pacific Railroads. The mines were successful in securing orders; but unable to fulfill them due to the re-occurring car supply problems. Labor strife was a common occurrence at the coal mines in Kansas, Arkansas and Missouri as the labor force was unionized. On May 17, 1908 the mines went on strike which lasted until May 26, 1908, with little change in contract terms. During this time period, the mine at Fidelity, Arkansas was flooded on May 13, 1908. (3) It would be necessary to pump out 60/75 million gallons of water to bring the mine back into production. Coupled with the strike, were the summer doldrums for selling coal.

By spring, 1909 the Stone City mine # 1 was in its final operating phase as coal veins had disappeared.(4) Midsummer 1909, the miners were back on strike; but Long-Bell mines were not affected. At this point sales and profitability looked favorable until the spring of 1910. In April 1910, the mines were struck again and were closed until September 21, 1910. Continuous labor troubles, profits now non-existent and the prospects of several mines were faced with closure due to dwindling coal veins, the company was forced to review its future in the coal business. In the spring of 1912, negotiations were started with John Mayer Coal Company, concerning the sale of all the coal properties, with the sale closing on July 18, 1912.(5) It was a great beginning but a difficult ending, with Long-Bell happy to be out of that venture. Certainly the constant labor difficulties contributed to the disenchantment with the coal properties. It also strengthened their resolve to avoid unionizing the sawmill properties.

Fidelity Coal Operations Early 1900's

Long-Bell was constantly looking for opportunities to dispose or lease cutover timberlands. The exploration for gas and oil deposits spread into Louisiana in the early 1900's with finding of oil in the central section of the state. Not long after the closure of The Globe Lumber Company, Yellow Pine, Louisiana in 1915, Long-Bell offered the entire tract of 58,000 acres for sale. (6) The asking price was $6.00 per acre without oil and gas rights, or $7.00 per acre with oil and gas included. Cut over timberland was considered worthless for anything other than mineral exploration as every producer had excess lands which needed to sold or turned back to avoid taxes. Long-Bell began to lease acreage for gas and oil exploration on the Globe property, with the announcement that Globe Oil Company had drilled a 300 barrel per day well and that Standard Oil was drilling a well adjacent to the Globe Company well. (7) Terms for leasing called for a fixed fee and royalty percentage to be paid to Long-Bell.

In 1916 Long-Bell offered the Noble cutover lands for exploration. This area derived from an investment Long-Bell had made with the R. L. Trigg Lumber Company, Noble, Sabine Parish, Louisiana, a few miles north of Shreveport, Louisiana. Interest in leasing 10/15,000 acres was being negotiated. A contract for an initial 5,000 acres was signed and attempts to re-activate an old well were underway. Efforts continued to lease the property, with the company announcing the successful lease of 5,000 acres to Marland Oil Company in the Globe cutover lands, with a payment of $100,000 dollars and royalties of 1/8 % of the successful development of a well. In subsequent developments where Long-Bell cutover land was involved, the company strived for a long term lease in their negotiations.

By 1934, when the company was involved with its reorganization, the financial report of S. C. Cronwall (a court appointed financial consultant) indicated that 210,468 acres were under lease, with 94,310 acres leased to Humble Oil and 21,848 acres leased to Sun Oil Company, with all of the acreage located in Louisiana and Texas. In addition sixteen other explorers leased 65,000 acres in Texas, Louisiana, Arkansas, Mississippi and Alabama. (8)

The results at the time were minimal in 1934; but it was pointed out in the report, that a significant find would take care of Long-Bell's financial difficulties. Long-Bell had considered the abandonment of their cutover lands to avoid the tax penalty but chose to maintain ownership due to the potential value of the mineral rights. In 1932 a new corporation, Long-Bell Minerals, was formed to manage the leases. Due to legal interpretations, the name was changed to Long-Bell Petroleum Corporation. By 1939 the company had leases on 588,000 acres of cutover land for oil and gas exploration possibilities, with 150,000 acres returning between $34,000 and $100,000 a year. During the period 1935-1943, the company received royalties or lease payments of $473,623 dollars. The period 1944-1951, leases covered 288,860 acres, receiving $2,548,412 and in 1953-1954, the company received $772,078 in revenue.(9) By aggressively offering the cutover land for exploration, Long-Bell realized a long term successful gain out of a potentially dismal situation with the opportunity a definite success.

A secondary plan within Long-Bell was to develop a program to market cut over land to small individual farmers. Nationally timber companies were concerned about disposing of cut over land. Millions of acres were involved and Environment concerns were strident enough that Congress was agitating about the over cutting of the timber. The area around Lake Charles, Louisiana had over 800,000 acres of cut over lands. There was considerable effort extended toward providing returning servicemen from World War I with land for farms and cut over land was the most likely source. The South was a rural economy with sawmill laborers coming from the farms and the company had thousands of acres of land not suitable for gas and oil exploration. They were anxious to sell the properties in order to avoid paying taxes. Long-Bell had developed an experimental farm located close to De Ridder, Louisiana to demonstrate the ability to grow local crops on soils left behind from the logging process. Grapefruit, Satsuma oranges, Pecans were planted, along with many other crops. The results obtained from the farm were published in local farm journals, newspapers and "The Long-Bell Log". The obvious intent was to influence potential purchasers of cut over land that the properties were suitable for farming. On July27, 1915, J. D. Tennant reported to the Long-Bell Board of Directors concerning a study on marketing cut over land. After reviewing several plans and alternatives, the Board consensus was that the selling of these properties was best done internally within the company.

Under the direction of T. H. Davis, properties were selected, surveyed and developed into 20, 40 and 80 acre tracts, with roads being laid out and developed. In the fall of 1915, Long-Bell invited F. W. Cornwall of J. Walter Thompson Advertising Agency to view the properties to be offered for sale and solicit his opinion as to the salability of land. Negotiations were conducted with Mr. Cornwall and concluded that J. Walter Thompson Agency would conduct the promotion of the land sales, with an advertising campaign to begin January 1, 1916. (10) As of January 8, 1916, a new corporation was formed, Long-Bell Farm Land Company.

Sales activity began early in 1916 and by May, 1916, 5000 acres had been sold, with expectations of increased sales in the near future. Selling price for the offered acreage was $12.00 to $20.00 per acre, with the majority of the sales at $16.00 per acre. Optimism continued as sales of 10,000 acres had been sold at an average of $14.26 per acre.(11) Long-Bell continued to increase the price of farm land lots, seeking $25.00 an acre by October, 1916. However by September 1917, farm land sales stagnated. On February 26, 1918 a Board of Directors discussion on whether to continue the program surfaced. The World War I excess profit tax burden was suggested as being burdensome to the program. Although management comments indicated dissatisfaction with the progress of the program, the 1920 Annual Report for the Long-Bell Farm Land Corporation, shows an operating profit of $45,508.59 which was a reasonable return for the time period.

While the effort was made, the long term results could not be considered a success. Total sales for the Farm Land Corporation were less than 15,000 acres. The 1920 Annual Report indicates that the corporation was carrying a debt owed by purchasers of $938,271. (12) Financial crisis in the late teens and early 1920's would see sizeable acreage returned to Long-Bell for non-payment of the land. The program eventually fell into disuse. Long-Bell would retain most of the cut over land for mineral rights development. During the depression of the 1930's 100,000 acres were abandoned by Long-Bell for tax purposes. In Texas, Long-Bell sold 73,800 acres to the United States government for inclusion in The Angelina National Forest at $2.93 per acre. Long-Bell made a noble effort; but one destined to be only a mediocre success. Soil conditions would prove to be marginal for farm purposes. Future success would prove to be in growing timber.

S. S. Angelina Loading at Beaumont, Texas

With the advent of World War I, the United States government developed an aggressive program to build Wooden Ships, as replacements for ships lost to hostile action by German Submarines. The program initiated in 1917, called The Emergency Fleet Corporation was to own and operate the ships to be built. The plan envisioned building 200,000 tons of ships per month, starting in October, 1917. The ships were designed to be 3,000 to 3,500 tons each, powered by oil or steam engines, capable of making 12 knots per hour. 800 t0 1000 ships were expected to be completed within the next fourteen to sixteen months. (13)

Wooden ships were chosen over steel, as time of construction was much less. The plan called for ship building facilities on the Atlantic Coast, Gulf Region and Pacific Coast. For the lumber companies in Texas and Louisiana, Port Arthur, Houston, Beaumont and Orange, Texas were the most suitable locations. Long-Bell began the investigation of Wooden Ship building in early 1917. By May, 1917 The Board of Directors had reached the conclusion that it would be a profitable venture and instructed L. L. Chipman to proceed to Washington D. C. to contract the building of one or two ships. A new corporation was designated as the Long-Bell Trust Company. The incentive to enter into a new totally unrelated business was the level of profit generated from each ship. The contract to build Wooden Ships guaranteed prompt payment for labor and materials, plus $20,000 profit for a ship's hull, or $40,000 if machinery is installed and the vessel was ready to sail. The government had guaranteed payment within 15 days upon presentation of charges, far better than normal retail or wholesale trade. (14)

Long-Bell constructed a ship building facility at Port Arthur, Texas and contracted to build at least four ships during the program. The governments program was not without problems, as large timbers required in the ship building could not be supplied by all mills in the program. The Southern Pine Emergency Bureau responsible for the program was able to re-distribute the orders among the mills to relieve the situation. Rail car supply problems, always troublesome to Southern sawmill operators took its toll on delivery schedules. Once again the government stepped in to place a priority on ship building material. (15)

A sizeable benefit from the ship building program and other war related efforts was a dramatic increase in asking prices for lumber. On the average, price levels increased to $12.00 per thousand board feet, starting in 1915, up to $14.00 in 1916 and spiraling upward in 1917. The average price for common dimension lumber peaked at $26.00 per thousand board feet, the highest level on record, with B@Better grade flooring selling at $32.50 per thousand board feet. The price of flooring was at $20.00 the year previous. In 1918 the federal government, over the protest of Southern Lumbermen, fixed the price of lumber at slightly less than the 1917 level. (16)

With the generous benefits of higher prices, came higher labor costs, as daily labor rates increased from an average of $ 1.75 to $ 2.50 per day. This was a one third increase in wages. Long-Bell certainly benefited from the ship building and other government inspired programs, generating excellent profits for the company. Long-Bell shipped over 11.5 million board feet of lumber to government sources during the war period.

The fifth category of opportunity for Long-Bell outside the standard business of producing and selling lumber was the entry into production of Naval Stores. Naval stores are the derivative of crude gum "Oleorein" that comes from living trees, stumps and dead wood.(17) Long-Bell utilized the trees in their forests, Loblolly, Short Leaf and Long Leaf pine. The practice of collecting gum from Pine trees called for scarifying the tree, allowing sap to drip into a metal cup. The sap would be then collected and processed in a still, where the turpentine would be separated from Rosin. The term Naval Stores is usually limited to include Turpentine and Rosin; but also include Pine Tar, Pine Oil and Rosin Oils. Long-Bell entered the Naval Stores business in the early 1900s, leasing timber land to Turpentine companies. Long-Bell operated Naval Stores operations at Quitman, Mississippi, Longville, Bon Ami, Hoy, Ludington and Woodworth, Louisiana, and Bannister and Doucette, Texas. In the 1908 Annual Meeting notes listed two companies, Long-Bell Naval Stores and Texas and Louisiana Naval Stores Company, as doing business in the product. By the mid teens of 1900, business transactions would be conducted as Long-Bell Naval Stores, headquartered at Doucette, Texas. Long-Bell would contract with collectors of crude gum for a five year period ahead of logging the timber.

Profits from the Turpentine and Resin operations were generally modest, ranging annually from $100 to $200,000. (18) This was a good return, considering little effort was being expended by Long-Bell, other than management negotiation and oversight. In 1918 the Long-Bell operations collected 31,040 barrels (17,520,000 pounds) of Rosin and 518,164 gallons of Turpentine. The year 1919 the volume increased in both product categories; but this would be the high point of the company's involvement. (19)

The ability to be involved in other products added considerable profit to Long-Bell companies. This was Indicative of the constant pursuit of opportunities for making a company profitable and reaching for growth in areas on the periphery of their main core business.

References:

(1) Robert Alexander Long A Lumber Man of The Gilded Age Lenore K. Bradley
        Page 29 and 50

(2) Long-Bell Board of Director Meeting Notes, October 22, 19 07

(3) Long-Bell Board of Director Meeting Notes, May 19, 1908

(4) Long-Bell Board of Director Meeting Notes, December 12, 1908

(5) Long-Bell Board of Director Meeting Notes, July 18, 1912

(6) Long-Bell Board of Director Meeting Notes, January 14, 1913

(7) Long-Bell Board of Director Meeting Notes, August 22, 1915

(8) S. C. Cronwall Report Re-organization of the Long-Bell Lumber Company,
        December 30,1932

(9) Long-Bell Financial Report, 1954

(10) Long-Bell Board of Director Meeting Notes, December 2, 1915

(11) Long-Bell Board of Director Meeting Notes, August 23, 1916

(12) Long-Bell Farm Land Corporation Annual Report, 1920

(13) Sawdust Empire,   Robert S. Maxwell and Robert D. Baker, Page 125

(14) Long-Bell Board of Director Meeting Notes, May 16, 1917

(15) Sawdust Empire,   Robert S. Maxwell and Robert D. Baker, Page 187

(16) Sawdust Empire,   Robert S. Maxwell and Robert D. Baker, Page 190

(17) Trees 1949 Yearbook of Agriculture Naval Stores The Industry, Page 286

(18) Long-Bell Board of Director Meeting Notes, February 8, 1916

(19) The Long-Bell Log, April 1920, Page 20

Chapter 7

THE COMPANY STORE

With the rapid expansion into lumber production, Long-Bell was faced with building a community as well as the mill. Housing, water, electricity, schools and a store or commissary were required before the mill was operating. The saw mill workers in the South were totally at the mercy of the mill operators. The employee rented his house, purchased his groceries and clothing at the company store and depended on the company for his job. Wages were minimal during the period 1850's through the beginning of World War I. There was improvement during the War; but soon slipped back. The worker was seldom out of debt to the company.

Long-Bell had a store in every community where they had mill operations. Communities where a mill had been purchased usually had commercial facilities competing with the company but company stores were opened and considered a success. Company store operations usually charged 10/15% higher than competing stores, yet maintained their profitability, and in many locations the employees were paid in company script or coins and the only place that would redeem the script at face value was the company store facility. Attempts to sell the script at banks or other locations resulted in a steep discount on the value of the script. There wasn't any way to avoid the hold that the company had on the employee

The company store was the social center of the community. The store or commissary as it was also known supplied almost all of the employee's needs. The stores varied in size, depending on the local population but also catered to those not in the employ of the company. Store management prided itself in the selection of items stocked. Certainly in the larger communities the items carried was quite varied. The stores operated as a semi independent business, in an attempt to keep competition from moving in to town, offering with pride a store, second only to that of a major city.

Grocery Department, Fidelity Store, Scammon, Kan.   Fidelity Store at Stone City, Kan.   Exterior View of Fidelity Store, Scammon, Kan.
Dry Goods Department, Fidelity Store, Stone City, Kan.   Grocery Department, Fidelity Store, Stone City, Kan.

VIEWS OF MINES AND STORES OWNED AND OPERATED BY THE FIDELITY LAND & IMPROVEMENT COMPANY.

The mercantile department was a major component of Long-Bell's cash income in the late teens and early 1920's. In 1918 the Long-Bell Log reported that over $3, 000,000 dollars was generated in sales volume from 18 stores. Volume of items stocked was impressive.

300 Tons Sugar	1000 Tons Flour
45 Tons Coffee	2 Tons Tea
500 Tons Meat	150 Tons Lard
45 Tons Candy	6000 Tons Feed
30,750 Pair of Shoes	15.000 Bolts of Cloth
6,800 Hats	1,750 Suits of Clothes

The above items would fill 200 rail cars, (40 tons per car) and make 5 good sized trains, canned goods, cereal, fresh vegetables, tobacco, work clothes, underwear and other staples would make another trainload. (1) In larger communities, a Drug store, Ice Cream Parlor, Butcher Shop, Hotel, a Hardware Store or in the case of Ryderwood, Washington, a tavern, would all be part of the community. Long-Bell company stores were often the community center, where the employees and their families would gather. The DeRidder store operated an ice plant which could produce 64 tons of ice at a time. The ice plant furnished ice to Bon Ami, Ludington and Longville communities as well as several competing saw mill towns in the area. In 1905, the company operated seven general stores, four, being adjacent to sawmills, two were located at coal mining properties of the company and one was located at Thomasville, Indian Territory. In 1903 Long-Bell had $102,943. invested in its mercantile operations, nearly the same amount as invested in the coal operations and only $ 50,000 dollars less, than the entire investment in the retail yards.(2)

The average investment in 1905 was $113,700, with total sales of $563,000 and purchases of $436,000. By 1919, the average investment per store was $850,000, total sales of $4,000,000 and purchases of $3,280,000. (3) Profit generated seemed well worth the effort. Company results for 1920 show a contribution of $1,555,386 for wholesale merchandise and $4,712,000 for retail merchandise. A little more than 8% of the total company sales of $ 51,248,000 for the year.

The Company stores were managed by F. H. Bester, who joined the company in 1901 as a manager of one of the stores. He soon became manager of the entire chain of stores and remained in this capacity until he retired in 1948. He was succeeded by Fred G. Schweitzer in 1948, who had been involved with the company stores since 1919 at DeRidder, Louisiana. He spent time at Weed and Longview, prior to being named assistant manager in 1946.

With the move West, Long-Bell's plan for the development of the Longview, Washington property called for building a modern city, organized in a manner similar to Washington, D. C. The mill plans called for employment of upwards of 4000 workers. The development of the community had to be organized in a manner that would accommodate employees, their families and new commercial businesses that would be attracted to the new location.

Long-Bell had a company store, The Columbia River Mercantile, built at the corner of Broadway and Commerce streets in the city of Longview, Washington. Recognizing that other stores would be built to compete with the " Merk" as it was called Long-Bell encouraged the competition. In order to coordinate the building of the city, Long-Bell formed the Longview Company, which was charged with the development and marketing of property, within the city boundaries. Within the structure of The Longview Company, was, The Longview Concrete Pipe Company, The Longview Bus Company, The Monticello Hotel, St. Helens Inn (lodging for single men), Longview Memorial Park and the Real Estate Company, selling and renting houses to employees and commercial development.

Long-Bell also had to build a community for the loggers, hired to cut the newly acquired timber. Ryderwood was developed, approximately 35 miles Northwest of Longview, with the community similar to the towns developed in the South. All of the facilities required in a mill community, were built for a town with 800 loggers. A company store, schools, houses, tavern (unusual for Long-Bell), community building and a dormitory for single loggers. This would be one of the first family logging camps for Long-Bell and one of the first in the Northwest.

When Long-Bell assumed control of Weed Lumber Company, the village had been developed. However when the mill was re-built in 1917, the expansion brought in many additional workers and the company would build a new enlarged store, hotel and houses for the workers .

By 1919/1920, the company had 18 stores. Due to the size of the communities involved, Longview and Weed stores were much larger than the others. The Longview Mercantile was a three story building plus a full basement. The building included everything a modern department store carried. A March 1936, Longview Daily News advertisement listed high quality furniture, Thor Washing Machines, Philco Radios, G. E. Refrigerators, curtains, men's suits and ladies apparel. Two page advertisements extol to all, the wide variety of items, including meat and groceries, for sale. The "Merk" was the largest department store in Southwest Washington and was the major profit center for the store group.

The depression years were extremely difficult for the company stores, yet they performed much better than the rest of the company. A listing of sales, profit, expense and net profit for the years 1926 through 1931 were positive, despite the difficult times

	1926	1927	1928	1929	1930	1931
Sales	$ 4,223.	$ 3,625.	$ 3,680.	$ 3,284.	$ 2,573.	$ 2,000.
Gross Pr.	$ 857.	761.	778.	719.	518.	390.
Expense	$ 549.	500.	505.	508.	436.	328.
Net Profit	$ 308.	261.	273.	211.	82.	63.
Avg. Inv.	$ 621.	606.	566.	594.	491.	400.
Acc. Rec.	$ 174.	180.	220.	241.	229.	196.
Tot. Avg. Inv.	$ 795.	785.	786.	835.	720.	430.

Percent Profit To Sales

	1926	1927	1928	1929	1930	1931
	7.30 %	7.20%	7.40%	6.27%	3.20%	3.12%

Merchandise Turnover per year

	1926	1927	1928	1929	1930	1931
	5.42	4.73	5.12	4.48	4.05	4.02

Number of Stores	1926	1927	1928	1929	1930	1931
	14	11	11	10	10	8

Net Profit of Western Stores in thousands

	1926	1927	1928	1929	1930	1931
	$ 173.	$ 144.	$ 174.	$ 133.	$ 53.	$ 50. (4)

In 1948 Long-Bell had six company stores, DeRidder, Louisiana, Longview, Ryderwood and Castle Rock, Washington, Weed and Tennant, California and Vaughan, Oregon. The Longview store was sold to The Bon Marche Corporation in 1950 and the Weed store was sold about the same time, with the rest being disposed of after the merger with International Paper ending a long tradition for the company.

Another view of the Long-Bell hardware store at Coffeyville

Hotel Bon Ami.

B. H. Smith, of Bonami, La.

The Commercial Hotel, at Bonami, La.

W. F. Ryder, of Bonami, La.

Group of Employees and Managers of the King-Ryder Lumber Company, at Bonami, La.

F. G. Kennesson, of Bonami, La.

The Doctor's Office, at Bonami, La.

Street Scene at Bonami, La.

Residence of B. H. Smith, at Bonami, La.

The Bon Ami School at Noontime, at Bonami, La.

Residence of W. F. Ryder, at Bonami, La.

VARIOUS VIEWS OF INTEREST AROUND BONAMI, LA., AND PORTRAITS OF PROMINENT MANAGERS OF THE KING-RYDER LUMBER COMPANY.

References:

(1) Long-Bell Log, August 1919, Page 1

(2) Robert Alexander Long, A Lumberman of The Gilded Age, Lenore K. Bradley , Page 50

(3) Long-Bell Log, May 1920, Pages 8/9

(4) Cronwall Report, Page 70

Chapter 8

CALIFORNIA AND OREGON

As Long-Bell and R. A. Long continued to prosper, it was time to look to the West for new investments. Through his former employee, George X. Wendling, R. A. Long was exposed to the Weed Lumber Company. The company located at Weed, California, was organized in 1903, with a capitalization of one million dollars. George X. Wendling had been a manager at Long-Bell retail yards in Cherryvale, Walnut and Caldwell, Kansas, starting in 1879 through 1887. In January 1888, he moved to California, entering into the retail lumber business in Fresno, California. This company catered to the fruit box business, supplying large volumes to this industry. In 1897 he assumed the management of The California Pine Box Association until 1899 when he returned to Wendling Lumber Company. (1) George X. Wendling became very successful, becoming involved in over twenty companies most of which were involved with lumber products.

Weed Lumber Company was formed March 14, 1903, with Abner Weed, President, R. F. Brown, Secretary and George X. Wendling, George Bittner, E. S. Moulton and Charles Sands as Directors. (2) It did not take long for Long-Bell to become aware of the opportunity to invest in Weed Lumber Company, purchasing a large block of stock in 1904, making Long-Bell the largest stockholder. Ownership of Weed Lumber Company fluctuated over the next several years. Abner Weed disposed of his holdings in the company in 1911, selling to George X. Wendling. (3) Charles Evans was General Manager at the time and company offices were located in San Francisco, California. Long-Bell continued to purchase stock in the company and by 1914 had gained control of the company. Long-Bell was not the only investor in Weed Lumber Company interested in gaining control. S. O. Johnson, a California and Eastern Oregon lumberman and cattle rancher had purchased a large block of stock in 1909 and was named Vice President in 1914, with George X. Wendling as President and L. Nathan an Secretary. By 1916, Long-Bell dominated the company and completed ownership in 1923. In 1926 Weed Lumber Company became the Weed Division of The Long-Bell Lumber Company. (4)

Abner Weed had been involved in logging and lumber manufacturing in Northern California since 1869, operating in the Ponderosa and Sugar Pine regions and for a short time logging in the Redwood District. He slowly built up capital to begin the operation of a small circular sawmill in Siskiyou County, California. He continued to search for the ideal location for a sawmill site with adequate timber resources. In 1897 he purchased 280 acres from Siskiyou Lumber and Mercantile which is now the site of Weed, California. Abner Weed then purchased a saw mill in Truckee, California with the intent of moving it to the Weed site. (5) His first task was to build a railroad spur from the Southern Pacific Railroad main line, which went from Sacramento to Ashland, Oregon, via Roseburg, Oregon on to Portland, Oregon.

98   AMERICAN LUMBERMAN.   July 1, 1904.

General View of the Saw Mill Plant of the Weed Lumber Company at Weed, Siskiyou County, California.

Long-Bell Log April 1941 Logging

Weed Lumber Company installed the mill purchased at Truckee, California and after a short time, built a new mill of the same capacity which would produce a combined volume of 125,000 feet of lumber a day. With the building of the sawmill, it was also necessary to construct lodging and eating facilities for the employees. By the time Long-Bell made its initial investment, the mill and community were thriving and a box plant had been added with a capacity of 60,000 feet per day in 11 hours. (6)

California lumber operations cutting Ponderosa and Sugar Pine during the 1880's through 1940's were concentrating on producing box material. Product mix was vastly different than the period after the World War II era. Box shook demand was huge as most every product was shipped in a wooden box. Ponderosa Pine mills produced more box shook than Mills in Oregon and Washington but the demand for all types of boxes was significant. Weed produced 60,000 feet a day in box material which was 50% of their production in early 1900's. The box plant produced special ordered sizes for box ends and sides, branded with the fruit company name and assembled flat. The boxes would be shipped to the field location and assembled on site for use. The first use of veneer in the West was for tops and bottoms of boxes. Companies such as Fruit Growers Express (a Sunkist Company) had three mills devoted to producing box shook.

With the increased capacity, the community of Weed continued to grow. In addition to the facilities built to accommodate the original crew, a store, post office, warehouse, boarding house, hotel and houses for supervisors were built. In 1904 the mill produced 40 million feet of lumber and box shook.

By 1907 sash and door production was added and in 1910 a planer mill, reflecting increased investment by the major stockholder. In 1911 a veneer lathe was added with a capacity of 10,000 feet a day with the product going into box tops and bottoms. Plywood was quickly added producing door panels of Ponderosa and Sugar Pine for the door factory, at the time 1000 door panels were being produced daily.

In addition to Weed Lumber Company, Long-Bell also invested in Stearns Lumber Company, Wendling, California, with a daily capacity of 200,000 feet of lumber including a box plant. The investment was made soon after the purchase of Weed stock and was still in effect in 1916. C. B. Sweet, Vice President and General Manager of Long-Bell apparently had a major ownership in the company but Long-Bell also participated.(7)

In 1917, it was decided to build a larger mill at Weed, replacing the two smaller mills, with a modern 250,000 foot capacity mill complete with power house. With Abner Weed's original premise of using wind for air drying, the Weed plant had three air drying yards, where green lumber production would move from the sawmill to the yards where it was stacked by hand using small lumber stickers between each layer for air flow separators. This was a standard operating procedure for Pine mills and probably for some Fir mills but not used to any degree for mills close to water shipment capability. Air drying was obviously a slow process taking 30/60 days to dry lumber down to the acceptable moisture content. The Weed mill did have some dry kilns within the old mill complex; but new kilns were added to speed up the turnover of the air dried stock especially for sash and door lumber. Kiln drying usually took 36/48 hours depending on size and thickness. The stacking yards at Weed were phased out in 1945. (8)

With the construction of the new mill in 1918, with a capacity of 250,000 feet per eight hour day, four head rigs were installed. It wasn't long before the mill ran two shifts per day. In 1922, the powerhouse was expanded. As with all sawmills built in this era, the waste burner was utilized and continued in use until 1931, when a terrific windstorm packing winds of 95 miles an hour blew down the existing burner. At that point all refuse from the mill was diverted to the powerhouse and the burner dismantled. Excess power was generated over what was needed to run the mill and steam for the dry kiln with the excess power being sold to the local power grid, generating additional revenue for the mill. (9)

By 1919, Long-Bell employed 750 men and women in the mill not including the woods crew. As with many industrial plants in the west, the crew was a mixture of nationalities. A, 1914 payroll roster listed 424 whites, 356 Italians and 89 Greeks, for a total of 869 employees. In 1923, the payroll listing shows out of a total of 1263 employees, 62 women, 723 white, 272 Italians, 30 Greek, 55 Mexican and 121 Blacks. Italian immigrants began to flow into Northern California in the mid 1800's, possibly as a result of the gold rush. Seeing opportunity in the timber camps, the influx of Italian workers grew, moving from one camp or mill to the next. Black workers were recruited from Louisiana mills as they began to close. Beginning with 5 Black employees in 1918, the numbers increased especially in 1922, when the Weed mill went on strike. Long-Bell actively recruited black workers, paying the initial cost from Louisiana to Weed, with the proviso that the company was paid back for the cost. In the mid 20's, Weed had over 1000 black citizens living in the town. It should be noted, that by the 1920's, women began to work at the mill. This was not unusual in the west coast lumber industry. (10)

Company housing worked on a caste system of sorts as management lived on Nob Hill, foremen, office workers and department heads lived on Main Street, Gilman Avenue and Camino Row. Sawyers, Saw Filers and Mill Wrights lived on Liberty and Shasta Avenue. Stringtown and Rabbit Flats were reserved for common labor, two streets for Italian families but most lived on company land in camps A, B and C, Mexican workers in Camp D and Blacks in Lincoln Heights, homogenous, yet segregated. (11)

At one time the logging railroad for Weed extended for 170 miles including spur logging track. Long-Bell had a special arrangement with the Southern Pacific Railroad, which relieved the company of main line railroad construction. By 1956 all of the major blocks of company timber had been logged by rail and the conversion to truck hauling began. With the acquisition of cutting rights of Hearst Publishing timber south of Weed in the early 1950's, all of the logs were trucked to a rail reload on the McCloud rail line which connected to the Southern Pacific for delivery to Weed. (12)

In 1960, investment in a new planning mill and other improvements occurred. Elimination of the log pond and conversion to dry land sorting was introduced. Utilizing a Timber Jack tractor to unload trucks and put logs into the mill began. The green chain was taken out and a mechanical drop sorting was installed. Labor problems seemed to be few and far between at Weed until the late teens. As the mill became more sophisticated and departmentalized, labor problems began to surface. The operation at that time consisted of the sawmill/green chain, stacking yards, lath mill, plywood plant, door plant, box plant and window sash plant. The Weed facility was a part of Long-Bell's success and history from 1904 through 1981, when the complex was shut down. Virtually every type product sold was produced including some unique to Weed alone. Commodity lumber products, Plywood, Treated, Doors, Windows, Boxes and Lath all contributed to the mills success. With the modernization of the mill, emphasis was directed to the cutting lines and Sash and Door plant. The majority of the mill employees worked in these facilities.

One product category, Cut Stock, has had little mention; but with the demise of wooden boxes, other uses for small pieces of lumber were found selling into the industrial wood parts market. Even in this day of plastic and other competitive products, wood parts are still a factor. An area Long-Bell excelled in was the toy industry. During the 1960's, Fisher Price, Mattel and Play Skool, purchased 500 to 600 carloads of wooden machined parts for their assembly lines. In addition kitchen cabinets, unpainted furniture and ironing boards were but a few of the items produced at Weed. (13)

Wherever Long-Bell operated, they usually had arrangements with other producers for purchase of finished product. In the Pine country of Oregon and Northern California their first contract was with Klamath Manufacturing, where they furnished the mill 100,000 feet of logs a day. It is a safe assumption that the lumber output was purchased by Long-Bell, possibly as a way for the mill to help pay for the logs. In 1909 Weed Lumber Company purchased Big Basin Lumber Company, Klamath Falls, Oregon which was mainly a retail yard; but did have a planning mill in conjunction with the yard.(14) Long-Bell operated The Shaw Lumber Company, Klamath Falls, Oregon, from 1935 until 1942 when the Southern Pacific Railroad took it over. This occurred after a Timber contract with Kesterson Lumber Company was canceled. Long-Bell operated a saw mill at Dorris, California, from 1936 until 1945. In 1950 the company purchased a mill at Etna, California, Sugar Creek Lumber Company, which cut 16 million a year. The mill was located about 70 miles North and West of Weed, and shipped the entire volume as green lumber to the mill at Weed for processing. This mill operated until the late 60's or early 70's. In addition they operated the Huff mill in Scotts Valley during the 1960's, operating similar to the Etna Mill. (15)

Although not close to the Southern Oregon timberlands, R. A. Long invested substantially with a group of Western lumbermen to acquire Ponderosa timberland in the Prineville, Oregon area. In 1922 a diverse group of sawmill operators formed Ochoco Timber Company with the intention of building a mill at Prineville, Oregon. The founders were R. A. Booth, Booth- Kelly Lumber Company, Phillip Buckner, Collins Pine/ Ostrander Lumber Co. and O. M. Clark, Clark- Wilson Lumber Co. (16) The 1929 depression stalled any attempt to build the mill, as the original investors defaulted on the timber purchase, returning the mortgage to Northwest National Bank, Minneapolis, Minnesota. It wasn't until 1938 that a different set of partners formed to build the mill. R.A. Long may have been involved early on as a silent investor, as 1928 financial records show R. A. Long properties with an investment of $ 250,000 in Ochoco Timber Company. R.A. Long's investment was made later in the 1920's and was safe from loss in the default. Well after the death of R. A. Long, new investors came together in 1937, to build the mill. On January 25,1938, the new group formerly organized with W. W. Clark (Clark and Wilson), E. S. Collins (Collins Pine/ Ostrander), A. C. Dixon (Booth-Kelly), W. E. Lamm (Lamm Lumber) and J. D. Tennant (Long-Bell) with Tennant being elected President. 1,000 shares were issued in the new company with R.A. Long, holding 501 shares. Ochoco Lumber Company was to buy timber from Ochoco Timber Company.

Logging Operatons, Tennant, California

The mill started up September 6, 1938 and shipped 21 million board feet of lumber during the year. Capacity was in the 60 to75 million board foot range. The mill ran as Ochoco Lumber Company until 1982 when it was dissolved and ran as a limited partnership. Financial records show R.A. Long properties holding 650 shares of Ochoco stock into 1950. J. D. Tennant played a key role in Ochoco Lumber until he died in 1949. The Ochoco stock was liquidated October 9,1950 with a dividend of $8,881.95 and it appears that Mr.Long's estate was the investor, not Long-Bell.(17)

As Long-Bell slowly disappeared from lumber production, the management and crew at Weed and other pine operations could hold their heads high knowing they materially added to the company's profit. It should be noted that the Weed area still provides employment in the wood products industry. Roseburg Forest products purchased the mill site from International Paper. Starting in 1983, Roseburg Forest Products operates a Veneer mill at Weed, California, employing about 150 people, 108 years after the mill first began.

With the purchase of an interest in the Weed Lumber Company in 1904, Long-Bell was about to open up a new experience in logging and manufacturing of Ponderosa Pine, Sugar Pine and Douglas Fir. Logging in Northern California and Southern Oregon would be somewhat different than the Southern states. Timber grew in open stands similar to Southern Pine; but it was much larger and terrain would be much more severe.

The LOG of Long-Bell

EARLY MORNING SCENE AT TENNANT, CALIF. WOODS CREW GOING TO WORK

Early day logging was by high wheeled carts powered by horses or oxen. With the construction of the Portland to Northern California railroad in 1887, logs would move to the mill via the railroad. In 1902, Weed built a logging railroad to the Northeast of the mill in an area called Sheep Rock a few miles off the main railroad and continued to expand the line up to Goose Nest Mountain by 1908 which was about halfway to the Oregon border from Weed. With the completion of the Southern Pacific line from Weed to Klamath Falls in 1909, a new area was opened up for logging. The logging site was to the East of Weed on the Northern and Eastern slopes of Mt. Shasta. (18)

The Weed operation made use of the railroad for moving logs until 1956. Great usage of the Southern Pacific railroad enabled Long-Bell /Weed to establish a string of logging camps which connected to the mainline via woods railway spurs. An agreement reached between Weed Lumber Company and the Southern Pacific gave the Southern Pacific access to all railway spurs within 40 miles of Weed, with the railroad covering the cost of the spur lines within this area, a good arrangement for both parties. As logging was being completed at Goose Nest mountain added railroad spurs were built at Grass Lake and Abner, California, tapping the timber which would have been on the north side of highway 97, going toward Klamath Falls, Oregon.

Pulling the logs up to the rail spur was done by horse and oxen teams consisting of 4, 6, or 8 or more animals using high wheel carts. In the early years, around 1900, logs were loaded on cars using horses and a pulley system but by 1909 this gave way quickly to Donkey engines. Horses were used in the Weed operations well into the 1920's, pulling the logs to where they could be coupled to the high wheels or a "Clyde (ground skidder). By 1915 the Clyde Universal ground skidder and the McGiffert loader were being used in the Goose Nest Mountain area. (19)

Logging operations switched to the south side of highway 97 with one of the first camps located out of Morrison, California, about 18 miles by rail from Weed. The spur lines were all built to main line specifications, so there would not be a need to transfer the logs. The first camp was almost due north of Weed and several miles from the main line. Logging was being done on the slopes of Mt. Shasta and had one camp with two Clyde ground skidders, two swing boom loaders and a high wheel camp. Another camp at Murphy, California was 12 miles up the main line from Morrison, California and had 2 Clyde ground skidders. The third camp was located at Ester, California a few miles from Murphy, CA. and was logging 100,000 feet a day for delivery to Klamath Manufacturing, Klamath Falls, Oregon. At the Bray wye, a new rail spur was being built which would become the main source of timber for the Weed mills for years to come. (20)

The town of Tennant, located on the Eastside of Mt. Shasta in 1920, was established as the headquarters for logging the Weed timber. The town was named after J. D. Tennant, a vice president of Long-Bell. This operation had 12 locomotives used in hauling logs from various spurs to the main line of the Southern Pacific. Similar to Ryderwood, Washington, it had all the required facilities to house feed and care for the employees. Tennant had 100 houses, a rooming house for 100 single men, cookhouse, community hall, school, power plant machine shop and store. In 1928, camp one was established about 40 miles east of Tennant. It was later replaced, with a new camp one, which operated until 1954. (21)

By the 1920's Caterpillar tractors began replacing horses hauling logs to the skidders/ loaders. Steam shovels would replace the stiff booms at some landings. Trucks for hauling logs would appear on the scene but were of little interest to Long-Bell until the 1950's. Electric Chain Saws were introduced in the 1940's, using the Caterpillar tractor generator for power.

In 1923 Western logging operations were fully mechanized. A steam skidder was purchased from Willamette Iron and Steel, Portland, Oregon for operation in the Weed logging operation. The skidder mounted on two 50'rail cars, had the ability to yard in logs and load logs on to rail cars at the same time. A 50' mast simulated a spar tree. Empty rail cars would move under the skidder and it had the ability to be moved to a new setting quickly.

In addition to being long distances from the mill, logging in Northern California and Southern Oregon was often located in steep terrain. Building railroads into timber often required switchbacks and steeper grades. Long-Bell timberland was scattered across Siskiyou, Modoc and Shasta Counties in California and Klamath and Lake Counties in Oregon, for a total acreage in the mid 1920's of 264,000.

With the initial purchase of the interest in Weed Lumber Company, Long-Bell acquired 63,000 acres of Pine Timberland estimated at 1.2 billion feet. In conjunction with the purchase of the Ryderwood tract in 1918, Long-Bell also made a series of purchases for the Weed operation. 86,418 acres were bought in Klamath and Lake County, Oregon, known as the Reservation tract. Subsequent purchases were made up through 1922 adding 70,920 acres in Siskiyou county, California and 41,348 acres in Klamath County, Oregon, with an additional 2300 acres added in 1927 in Siskiyou and Modoc Counties, California. Long-Bell also had a contract with Walker Holdings, a Minnesota company, on 14,272 acres of timberland, which was relinquished in 1932. This would complete the timber acquisitions until 1956 when the Hearst timber was added.(22)

Some of the timberlands purchased in Oregon proved to be too far from the mill or too expensive to log. The timber known as the Reservation tract was situated North of Klamath Falls, along the East side of Klamath Lake and East of Klamath Falls toward Bly and Lakeview, Oregon. Long-Bell sold 600 million feet to Lamm Lumber Company, who had a mill on the North end of the lake in the mid 1920's. Lamm Lumber logged the purchase for several years until the contract was cancelled. The Lamm Lumber Company claimed excessive rot in the uncut timber, but the suspicion was that financial troubles were the real reason. In the early 1930's the remaining timber from the original sale was sold to Kesterson Lumber Company who then logged it for several years. While not clear as to the reason other than the depression, Kesterson cancelled the contract and Long-Bell took back the remaining timber, purchasing Shaw Lumber Company, Klamath Falls, Oregon to utilize the timber from this tract. They ran the mill until 1942 when the Southern Pacific Railroad took it over.(23) At a later date the remaining timber in the Reservation tract was sold to Weyerhaeuser Timber Company, including the sawmill. It was reported, that this transaction was completed by passing the value of the sale to what was still owed on the Ryderwood tract, in Cowlitz and Lewis Counties in Washington, without cash being used. In addition, Long-Bell sold 40,000 acres to Weyerhaeuser in 1928 from their lands in Oregon indicative of Long-Bell's tight cash position. (24)

Long-Bell Operations at Weed, California

Beginning, August, 1927 the Weed division adopted a system of select cutting, intending to leave all trees 18' and under. A forester was assigned to the woods to pick trees for cutting and to carry out the application of general forestry. Previous to this, the foreman of each logging side selected the trees to be cut. Within the forest industry, especially on the west coast, agitation for better forest practices had been evident for several years. Issues pertaining to forest taxation, fire protection and reforestation were important to owners of large areas of timberlands. Long-Bell was among the early practitioners of tree planting, establishing tree nurseries at Ryderwood in 1926 and Weed in 1929. (25)

Fire patrols were started in the early 1920's and results indicated this contributed to minimal losses. Slash was not piled during this time period; but frequent firebreaks were cleared and burned along roads and rail tracks. Close cooperation between logging companies, state forestry and the U.S. forest service assisted in keeping the fire danger under control.

Logging in the high mountains of the Sierra Nevada range, meant that logs must be hauled to the mill in 8 or 9 months to satisfy the needs of the mill, as the snow levels would be more than the loggers could cope with. Logs would be cold decked at the mill and in extreme cases at selected locations in the woods, though not a satisfactory solution as the logs would need to be moved twice. With snow levels of 13 to14 feet at 3000/4000 feet elevation or above, the ability to move logs from the woods was virtually impossible. Weed had a 35 acre dry sort yard and an 18 acre log pond, to accommodate the winter supply of logs. It would be necessary to accumulate 30 million feet of logs so the mill could work through the winter. (26)

Long-Bell Log May 1922 Weed Logging

As Long-Bell worked through the 30's and 40's, log trucks became an option for hauling logs to the mill. It would not be the main transportation method until 1956, when the rail system was shut down. At the height of the rail system, Long-Bell had a minimum of 130 miles of mainline track coming out of company lands, with spur track adding another 40 miles.

In 1956, with Tennant shut down, having cut the timber in the area, Long-Bell secured cutting rights to 20,000 acres of Pine and Douglas Fir from the Hearst Corporation, located on their tree farm " Hearst Wyntoon" in the coast range of Siskiyou and Shasta counties along the McCloud River. The site, about 35 miles south and east of the mill site, with the logs trucked to a reload on the McCloud railroad and would reach Weed via the Southern Pacific railroad. The purchase would add substantial volumes to the timber supply of the Weed mill. (27)

By the late 50's and early 60;s Long-Bell had begun to use contract loggers in some areas including Klamath and Scott Valley which was west of Weed in the Trinity Mountain's ; but company loggers were still working the Hearst tract. By 1964 contract loggers were cutting in the Goose nest Mountain area where the company first started logging 60 years before. Contract loggers were also supplying logs to a mill at Etna, California, which Long-Bell had purchased in 1950.

The Long-Bell Division of International Paper operated until December, 1981 when it closed the entire operation. It is likely that dwindling raw material and severe market conditions of the early 80's contributed to the closures. The log deck available at the time of closure was sold and the timberlands were sold in 1982 to Fruit Growers Supply Company, who sell timber in the Northern California region. (28) It should be noted that a McGiffert loader and a Clyde logging skidder were donated to the logging museum, which is located north of Klamath Falls, Oregon.

Resources

(1) Tree To Trade in Yellow Pine, American Lumberman, July 2, 1904, Page 75

(2) American Lumberman, June 17, 1905, Page 35

(3) American Lumberman, March 4, 1911

(4) American Lumberman, January 10, 1914

(5) The Siskiyou Pioneer, The Weed Edition, The Siskiyou County Historical Society Page 57

(6) The Siskiyou Pioneer The Weed Edition, The Siskiyou County Historical Society   Page 57

(7) The Siskiyou County Historical Society E-Mail April 10, 2012

(8) The Siskiyou Pioneer, The Weed Edition, The Siskiyou County Historical Society Page 85

(9) The Siskiyou Pioneer, The Weed Edition, The Siskiyou County Historical Society Page 40@41

(10) The Siskiyou Pioneer, The Weed Edition, The Siskiyou County Historical Society Page 32

(11) The Siskiyou Pioneer, The Weed Edition, The Siskiyou County Historical Society, Page 80, 81

(12) The Long-Bell Log, 1956, Page 9

(13) The Long-Bell Log, April 1962, Page 4 & 6

(14) The Long-Bell Log, October 1929, Page 2& 3

(15) Siskiyou County Historical Society E- Mail April 10, 2012

(16) Timberman Magazine, June 1939, Page 36,38 &40

(17)   R.A. Long Personal property financial records, 1950 page 4, Stocks and Bonds

(18) The Siskiyou Pioneer, Weed Edition, The Siskiyou County Historical Society, Page 57

(19) The Siskiyou Pioneer, Weed Edition, The Siskiyou County Historical Society, Page 59

(20) Long-Bell Log, August 1920,   Page 7

(21   Long-Bell Log, January 1928, Page 1

(22) E. C. Cronwall Report, Page 77

(23) E. C. Cronwall Report,   Page 80

(24) Longview Daily News, January 4, 1928 Page 1

(25) Long-Bell Log, April 1928, Page 4 & 5

(26) Long-Bell Log, March 1964, Page 16 & & 19

(27) Long-Bell Log, June 1956,   Page 7

(28) Forest History Today, Citrus Fruit and Forests by Ted W. Nelson , Spring/Fall Issue, A publication of
       The Forest History Society Page 24 to28

Chapter 9

WINDOW AND DOOR PRODUCTS

The growth of Long-Bell in the late 1800's and early 1900's was benefited by rapid expansion of the railroad system, oil exploration and the general increase in population. In order to grow, the Long-Bell retail yard system needed to be ahead of their competition by providing quality products. Home construction was heavily oriented to wood based products and most of the interior finishing items (doors, windows and trim) were also produced from wood. The Sash and Door category provided the materials needed to complete the house.

Desirable raw material came from tight grained old growth timber and supplies were readily available from Southern Pine, Western Pine and Douglas Fir and Hemlock stands of timber. With window sash and door parts able to utilize short length material, shop grade lumber was the most suitable for this end use. Shop grade lumber was sawn lumber which had a clear segment of variable length surrounded by large knots or defects which would be cut out.

With the acquisition of a major stake in Weed Lumber Company in 1904, Long-Bell made a significant move toward rapid growth of the company. The acquisition allowed them to reach a sizeable market to windows and door producers on the upper Mississippi River in Iowa, Illinois, Wisconsin and Minnesota by supplying Ponderosa and Sugar Pine shop lumber, which replaced depleted sources of Northern White Pine.

Ponderosa and Sugar Pine quality closely matched that of White Pine, with soft textured lumber suitable for windows, doors and trim manufacture. Other specie worked well; but soft textured wood was preferred. The California mills offered a steady supply of shop lumber and fit production practices as the lower grades moved into the wooden box shook market.

In 1907, Weed Lumber Company built a window and door plant designed to convert a higher percentage of the mill cut into finished products. In 1908 a small veneer mill was built, primarily for the box plant; but veneer for door faces was selected out in the peeling process. By 1911 plywood was being produced, with 1000 door panels produced per eleven hour day.

The Weed Sash and Door plant was a major production unit at Weed Lumber Company. The Door plant produced 250 doors per hour, or 550,000 a year. The Window plant produced 200 windows an hour or 500,000 a year. Windows varied widely in style and size between different regions of the country and the Weed plant produced Western, New York, Philadelphia, Baltimore, Ohio and Richmond styles and sizes. Window production was usually to specific order as it was almost impossible to develop standards sizes. Doors were slightly different as door openings were more standard. The plant, which started up in 1909, employed 125 in 1921, cutting about 75,000 board feet per day, which included box shook volume. (1)

Long-Bell Log Window Glazing 1925

The cutting line utilized three separate grades of shop when cutting for window and door parts: #1 shop (approximately 80% recovery), #2 shop (60/70% recovery) and #3 shop (approximately 50% recovery). As wood parts for doors and windows were cut to size, they were machined and assembled according to the pattern or size desired. The windows were shipped unassembled, with all parts to a size bundled together. Doors were shipped assembled, about 1300 per carload. (2)

The Weed facility offered a wide variety of doors and windows. In Long-Bell's woodwork book, windows were offered in 2, 4, 8 or 12 light sizes and glazed to order. However the vast majority were shipped unglazed. Casement windows (pairs), transoms, French doors, leaded and art glass were offered in addition to regular windows. Doors were available in Ponderosa or Sugar Pine and patterns such as slat, louver, colonial, screen, cupboard, front and flush doors, plain or beaded glass, mirrored, Dutch and doweled doors. Available veneer species were Douglas Fir, Idaho White Pine, Birch, and Juana Costa. The Weed sash and door plant began to offer finger jointed window and door parts in the 1960's. This was done to extend the recovery of raw material. These parts were veneered over the joints to give the appearance of solid wood. While not a significant volume, it did utilize the short lengths of shop that would have gone into hog fuel.

Quality control was of utmost importance, as every piece was exposed to view. The people responsible for cutting, grading and inspecting, the final product, had to insure only first class products were shipped. In the case of doors, the final inspection was at time of loading.

With the opening of the window and door plant, Long-Bell was not able to control the sales of this product category because the original charter of the company gave this right to George X. Wendling, who also had the rights to sales of box shook and Plywood. Wendling and Nathan received a 5 % commission on the sales of these product lines.

Long-Bell made several attempts toward controlling the sales for windows and doors. On September 21, 1915 Long-Bell Board of Directors made a formal proposal to The Weed Lumber Company to transfer sales control to Long-Bell which the Weed Lumber Company declined. By 1917, Long-Bell had purchased enough Weed Lumber Company stock to effectively control the company. At the same time management changes were occurring at Weed Lumber Company. L. Nathan corporate secretary and partner of George X. Wendling, resigned, Charles Evans General Manager was relieved of his duties and replaced by E. H. Cox and J. M.White, current treasurer would be named assistant General Manager. The Long-Bell influence was taking hold.

In June, 1919 a proposal presented by John C. Haring, window and door sales at Weed Lumber Company, proposed that Long-Bell take over the sales of Windows and doors. (3) An agreement was reached giving Long-Bell a 5 % commission on product sales. In February 1920, a new department was established, with Long-Bell hiring experienced personnel from competing window and door companies. Distribution warehouses were developed at Enid, Oklahoma and Pittsburgh, Kansas with a new facility being built at Kansas City, Missouri to handle distribution west of the Mississippi River. Long-Bell went outside of their existing sales organization to hire a knowledgeable sales manager. Earl Kenyon was named head of the group, coming from Payne Lumber Company, Oshkosh, Wisconsin, major manufacturers of sash and doors. In 1920, Long-Bell added two experienced sales men, Walter Kautz, named manager of the Kansas City, Missouri facility and G. A. Scott who would assist Earl Kenyon in the organization of the department.(4)

In 1921, with the department continuing to grow, an additional distribution facility was added in Oklahoma City, Oklahoma and an additional salesman, J.E. Pennybaker, who coordinated the distribution network. By 1951, two additional distribution facilities had been added at McAlester, Oklahoma and Amarillo, Texas, bringing the total to six. This would signal a major shift for Long-Bell toward converting the retail yards to distribution facilities in key selected markets involved with all wood products, not just sash and doors.

With the Weed mill being a major supplier of sash and doors, a move was made to enter into the window glazing business. In 1922, Long-Bell built a window glazing plant at Fort Smith, Arkansas, which was adjacent to Harding Glass Company, a producer of window glass. Window sizes varied depending on the particular region being shipped to. Long-Bell was able to carry large stocks of the most standard window sizes. A good window glazer could produce approximately 500 windows a day. This proved to be a very successful investment for the company. The plant was still operating in 1959. (5)

In 1927 the company opened a Sash and Door distribution warehouse called a Service Station in Chicago, Illinois. With the prime purpose of stocking Sash, Doors, Windows and Factory products, being designed for quick shipment to meet market needs. A second facility was opened in Detroit, Michigan soon after the first one. The two facilities operated until 1931 when market conditions in both cities declined to the point where the service was not justified. Other distribution facilities in Oklahoma and Kansas remained in operation throughout the depression period. The North Kansas City warehouse which opened in 1920, operated until 1925. (6)

While emphasis on Ponderosa Pine for sash and door was predominant, Douglas Fir and eventually Hemlock were also utilized. With the opening of the Longview operation, a new supply of product was available. Douglas Fir developed large quantities of shop grade lumber suitable for windows, doors and window parts. In the case of Longview, the mill was not involved with the production of door and window parts, although the original plan for the Longview operation called for a door and window plant employing approximately 450 men. The factory, located on the West mill site, adjacent to the planning mill did produce some volume of door and window parts for Fort Smith, Arkansas. The factory was designed to supply industrial wood parts and for a long time, involved with Sears Roebuck in producing kitchen cabinets and other knockdown furniture, continuing into the 1960's even though the sawmill had closed.

With the conversion from wood to aluminum and plastic windows and doors, the production of sash and door took a downturn and with the closing of the Weed sawmill complex, Long-Bell/ I.P. closed the chapter on this highly profitable venture.

Long-Bell

California White Pine
DOORS
yet they cost no more than ordinary doors

Here are eight outstanding points of merit for Long-Bell all California White Pine Doors:

1—All California White Pine.

2—Not a combination of woods.

3—Made of selected materials by skilled men, under strict supervision, and with frequent inspections in the processes of manufacture.

4—Put together with straight-grained oak dowels and water-proof glue.

5—Will not check or split. Less liable to warp than doors of other woods.

6—Fewer coats of paint or enamel necessary; take paints and enamels with superior results.

7—Panels, all California White Pine, ⅜-inch, 3-ply laminated rotary cut veneer.

8—Sanded and ready for finishes.

ALL LONG-BELL DOORS BEAR THE TRADE-MARK — Long-Bell

LOS ANGELES

Long-Bell all California White Pine Doors can be painted, stained or enameled and, because of the nature of California White Pine, fewer coats are necessary to obtain beautiful effects.

An Exhibit of Beautiful
DOORS
See the free exhibit of Long-Bell all California White Pine Doors at
1109 LOEW'S STATE BUILDING
Open from 9 to 5

CALIFORNIA

A California White Pine door like this would be an article of usefulness and beauty in your home as long as the home stands. Nothing in your home is more conspicuous than the doors.

(No. 1 of the series.)

The Long-Bell Lumber Company
Los Angeles Office, 1109 Loew's State Building
TELEPHONE PICO 5645
If your dealer cannot supply Long-Bell doors, call our Los Angeles office and we will give you the names of dealers who have Long-Bell Doors in stock.

Page 11

89

Resources:

     (1) Long-Bell Log, January 1921, Page 25

     (2) Long-Bell Log , January   1921, Page 10

     (3) Long-Bell Board of Director Meeting Notes, June 25, 1919

     (4) Long-Bell Log, April 1919, Page 7

     (5) Long-Bell Log, April 1955, Page 4

     (6) Cronwall Report, Page 64

Chapter 10

COMMUNICATIONS

In this modern business world, consider doing your daily work effort without benefit of computer, fax, internet or adequate telephone service. The successful company operating in the late1880's to the 1920's existed mainly through the telegraph, mail and occasional telephone call. Long-Bell a highly successful lumber company, operated under these conditions. Orders taken by the company salesman, were mailed to Kansas City, processed and mailed to the mill or in extreme situations, telegraphed when special conditions warranted. All stock offerings or production reports were sent by mail, which usually took 7 to 10 days. With our present day high speed information gathering and dissemination, these conditions would be intolerable.

Long-Bell management believed in communicating to all who would listen, the customer, employees, mill communities and across the country. Besides the need for rapid interchange between Kansas City and the mills or salesmen, Long-Bell believed in keeping the building material trade well supplied with articles of mill accomplishments. The art of advertising Long-Bell products was initiated at the retail yard level, usually on an individual basis. This would have occurred in the 1880's and 1890's. As Long-Bell grew, trade journals were writing glowing accounts of the mills and key personnel. In 1900, the American Lumberman magazine published, an eighteen page, article about the company, detailing the key personnel, location of mills and retail yards and how the company was operated. (1) In 1904, the first publication of Tree To Trade In Yellow Pine, outlining, the 30 year history of Long-Bell, was published in the American Lumberman. This article went into much deeper in depth information than the 1900 article. This story encompassed 61 pages outlining mill activities, sales organizations and locations of retail yards including pictures of key personnel. The American Lumberman also had articles about R. A. Long, M. B. Nelson General Sales Manager and Joseph H. Foresman Manager of the Retail Yard system. (2)Occasionally, this would be underwritten by the company being featured.

The West Coast Lumberman, published in Tacoma, Washington and The Timberman Magazine, published in Portland, Oregon and other trade journalists who covered the West

Coast producers, often had information about Long-Bell, as the company had a purchasing office and concentration yard for Cedar Shingles in Tacoma in the late 1890's and early 1900's.(3)

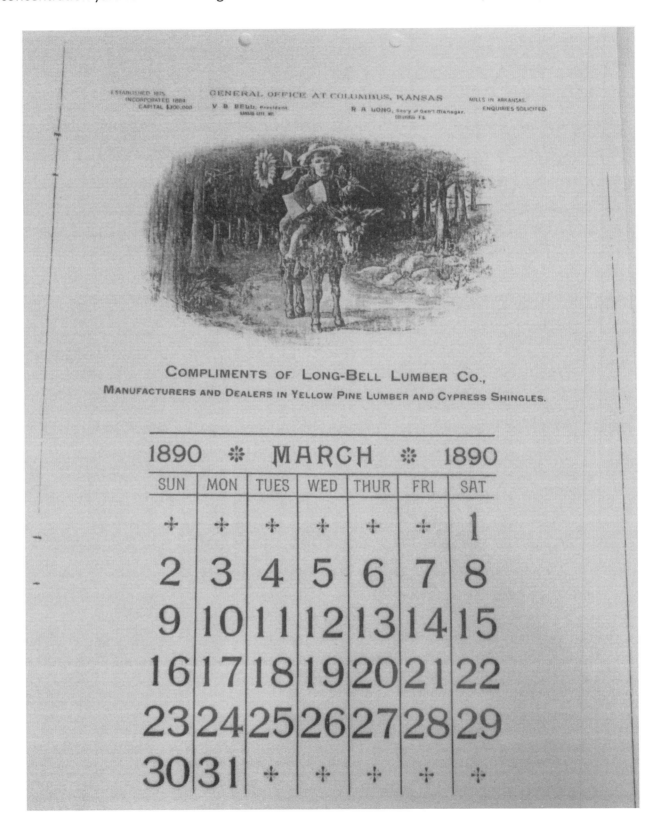

As Long-Bell grew in size and sales volume, the market for their product expanded rapidly. With a solid reputation to protect, the company expanded on two fronts, national advertising and trade marking its lumber products. With so many competing lumber producers from the South, Rocky Mountains, West Coast, Upper Middle West and New England, the customer had little idea where they could purchase quality products, which were consistent carload after carload. In 1919, Long-Bell was a pioneer in developing the trademark system. Each piece of lumber was end stamped with the Long-Bell trademark, to insure the customer that the company was proud of the product and was willing to stand behind it. This gave the salesman a tremendous base of support in selling consistent quality to the lumber dealer. Eventually trade marking became a universal tool for all of the major lumber producers. (4)

Product advertising has been a marketing tool for many years; but mainly at the local level and quite common in lumber trade journals. As early as the 1890's, trade journals used the advertisement to finance printing costs. Advertisements were simple and to the point. The West Coast Lumberman was one of these early journals being published from the late 1890's until the mid 1940's. Market comments by major region, Seattle, Portland, Tacoma, Chicago and other locations allowed the subscriber to stay in touch with what was happening to the market. The Timberman Magazine, published from the 1890's was a competing journal to the West Coast Lumberman and also provided commentary on current conditions in the industry, new machinery or process innovations and advertised items for sale within the timber community.

Long-Bell utilized this outlet to the fullest extent. However the need to reach out to new markets caused the company to establish a national advertising department in the late teens. The move was to drastically increase national awareness of the Long-Bell Lumber Company. The 1919 advertising campaign was designed to reach 211,915,105 readers. The advertisements were to be published in 259 issues of 30 individual magazines. Building, Technical and Farm oriented publications were familiar audiences at 8% and 39% of the total readership. However a new category of magazines was designed to have the greatest penetration. Long-Bell wanted to become a national name, recognized in all parts of the country. Magazines such as Saturday Evening Post, Literary Digest, Scientific America and Country Life were all selected to reach the casual reader at 51 % of the readership.(5)

National advertising was slanted toward quality, service, dependability and name recognition. The thrust was to cease being a Midwest lumber concern. With the investment being developed in Washington State and expansion in Northern California, new products would be coming on the market. The public and trade needed to be aware of the progress. The ability to sell trademarked and advertised lumber was an excellent selling tool for the company salesmen.

With the move into advertising and customer awareness of Long-Bell and the service it offered, the next step was merchandising products which displayed or enhanced the company name. Nail aprons, rulers, yardsticks and other items all emblazoned with the company name were quickly introduced, primarily through the company retail yards; but the wholesale customers were quick to take advantage of this selling tool. The one category that outsold all others was the building plan development. With World War I over and prosperity on the horizon, home ownership was achievable. A wide variety of building plans were developed, including farm buildings, which promoted company products such as lumber, treated, oak flooring, sash and doors. These items were a retail yard mainstay for many years.

As technology developed, business methods changed to keep up with the rapid pace. By 1922, lumber mills were using the telegraph to advise of shipment and occasionally to send a rush order to the mill. Telephone lines were improving and utilized to speed up communications. In the early 1900's a manager used a stenographer for dictating messages but by the late teens the Dictaphone was in wide usage. (6)

It is difficult to envision a forty million dollar company having only the telephone and telegraph for speedy communication. In 1922 metered mail was introduced and Long-Bell was quick to install the system. In 1926, the company installed the first national private wire printer and telegraph system in the country. The service ran between Kansas City, Longview and Weed, California operations, a distance of 2800 miles. The system operated at 35 words a minute, cutting communication time by at least 5 days. Operating a company of this size, dictated that the most up to date methods be employed in order to keep growing. While not competing directly with the industrial giants of the Middle West and East, it was a substantial coup to have developed this communication network. (7)

Also in 1926, the company took the next innovative step by installing equipment to send pictures over telephone lines. The ability to communicate quickly between a vast sales organization, mills scattered around the country and Kansas City, was extremely important. Being able to communicate with the mill "today" generated many valuable orders. (8)

As another important communication tool in 1919, Long-Bell began publication of" The Log of Long-Bell". The publication was designed to educate the employee and provide news about the company. Eventually each mill would have a correspondent, providing news of the mill and employees. This was the ultimate in communication as it was directed to every employee and their families. The "Log" was published monthly from 1919 through 1929, discontinued from 1930 to

1938 then began again in 1939 and ran into the early 1980's when it was absorbed into International Papers company publication. The Log, as it was known, covered virtually every subject considered relevant to the company, including expansion, personnel moves, education articles and individual family members. (9) A popular couple in the Kansas City office announce their engagement, a mill manager at Quitman Mississippi moving to a Western assignment is feted by his workers, a new baby at De Ridder, Louisiana all were noted in "The Long-Bell Log".

In 1920, Long-Bell published a new Tree to Trade Booklet. This publication followed the outline of a previous article; but updated to the present with details on new mills, products and updated methods of logging and manufacturing. Much had changed in the industry since the first article was written in 1904. New products such as Treated Lumber, Hardwood Lumber, Oak Flooring and Ponderosa Pine Sash and Door, Plywood all had been introduced by Long-Bell enhancing its position as a premier producer of lumber products. Tree to Trade was an expensive method of advertising. The research, writing and transforming the data into a successful sales tool was costly and time consuming, but it became a sought after publication within the lumber trade. (10)

Long-Bell continued to utilize the media to further its name and needs. When the decision to expand to the West was made, much was published in newspapers and magazines about the company plans. Every segment of the progress was reported by local and national newspapers. Land acquisitions, building the mills, developing the town, school, library and hotel were all documented throughout the Northwest and lumber trade.

As the Longview complex was developing into a functioning operation, workers were needed to staff the mill and purchase the houses being built in the Longview community. The National advertising campaign created in 1919 was directed toward attracting workers to the new city. Advertisements were placed in leading magazines of the era such as Saturday Evening Post, Literary Digest and others extolling the virtues of the area. R. A. Long and Long-Bell spent a tremendous amount of money developing the city. They had a great need to bring in workers, merchants and other businesses to help pay for this massive outlay. The advertisements were successful as the new city grew.

North~East South~West
you can know the lumber you buy

IN most markets—North, East, South, West—buyers can now obtain the four principal commercial woods bearing the Long-Bell trade-mark — Douglas Fir, Southern Pine, California White Pine and Southern Oak.

Douglas Fir is the newest addition to the lumber and timber products of this company. From new manufacturing plants at Longview, Washington, Long-Bell Douglas Fir is being shipped into markets accustomed to using this wood.

On any of these products—on many other lumber products—

the Long-Bell trade-mark signifies thorough care in manufacture, the skill resulting from nearly fifty years' experience as lumbermen, and the unusual pride of an organization in the sound building value their products give to home and industrial construction.

> Douglas Fir Lumber and Timbers; Southern Pine Lumber and Timbers; Creosoted Lumber, Timbers, Posts, Poles, Ties, Guard-Rail Posts, Piling; Southern Hardwood Lumber and Timbers; Oak Flooring; California White Pine Lumber; Sash and Doors.

Buy Identified Lumber

Ask Your Lumberman for Long-Bell Trade-Marked Lumber Products

THE LONG-BELL LUMBER COMPANY
R. A. LONG BLDG.   Lumbermen Since 1875   KANSAS CITY, MO.

Long-Bell
Trade-Marked LUMBER

KNOW THE LUMBER YOU BUY

Resources:

(1) American Lumberman, April 21, 1900, A Great Business Organization, Pages 27-45

(2) American Lumberman,July 2, 1904 From Tree To Trade in Yellow Pine, Pages 47-115

(3) West Coast Lumberman, February 1905, Page 291

(4) Long-Bell Log, January 1919, Page 4

(5) Long-Bell Log, January   1919 , Page 28

(6) Long-Bell Log, February 1924, Page 2

(7) Long-Bell Log, February 1926, Page 2

(8) Long-Bell Log, February 1926, Page 3

(9) Long-Bell Log, January   1919, Page 1

(10) From Tree To Trade, Long-Bell Lumber Company, 1920

Chapter 11

LONG-BELL - THE PLAN

When Long-Bell decided to purchase the Northwest tract of timber, in the late teens, a decision on where to locate the production facilities was required. Under the direction of Long-Bell's chief engineer, Wesley Vandercook, an extensive situation report was developed. Numerous investigations were made as to site consideration, logistics, logging practices, available labor, climate, transportation and other considerations.

In the present day business world of the 21'st century, business plans are mandatory and necessary to a successful operation; but in the late teens a plan of this magnitude was rare. The depth of the research on the Longview Plan and the manner in which it was presented, gives a clear idea how well based the Long-Bell organization was. The Northwest was a new area for Long-Bell to consider; but they knew little of the area and the operating problems involved. It cannot be said they were totally ignorant of the territory as they purchased lumber and shingles in large quantities for their retail yards and wholesale business.

The engineering review for the Longview operation was thorough and complex. Issues such as climate, river flow, ice in the winter, labor supply, hydro- electric power supply were all evaluated. When Long-Bell considered the move from the south, it had originally thought about separate mills for cargo and domestic markets. Sites were considered in the Astoria, Oregon area, the lower Columbia area (Cowlitz River) and the upper river area (Haydon Island near Portland, Oregon). Their long range plan considered that a large volume of lumber would be cut for the Export and East Coast markets. Locating a mill on navigable water where it would be served by ships plying the open sea's, was of prime importance. Being a long distance from the timber stands was not as critical, as towing costs were minimal. (1)

In the early part of the 1900's, with the opening of the Panama Canal markets on the East Coast and Gulf Region were opened up to West Coast lumber products. This market opportunity would remain positive well into the 1980's and 1990's. California would also be a major outlet by water, primarily by barge. The product in both markets was green lumber, eliminating the kiln drying process, reducing cost and speeding delivery to the marketplace.

When reviewing the desirability of constructing a new sawmill complex, the engineers considered all of the factors relating to the cost of construction in the West. Water containment dikes and dredging the river for ship loading were included as a portion of the review. Comparing the cost of construction of a new mill complex, with that of existing operations along the Columbia and Willamette, was also included.

The availability of labor was reviewed as to the quality and stability of the labor force. This would be a major factor in plant location as there would not be any black laborers available. Southern plants usually were staffed approximately 50% white and 50% black, although the percentage of black laborers varied depending on location. The company would also be facing a challenge with labor organizations. Another factor would be the use of women on the plant site. The fact that other companies employed women quickly drew their attention. (2)

When considering the layout of the logging operations, Long-Bell knew that the labor force was highly transient. While acknowledging that married men seldom fit into normal logging operations, there was evidence that a few companies made use of them. The end result was to site their logging camp" Ryderwood" close to the actual logging and build housing for families. Long-Bell would eventually have over 800 employees at Ryderwood and about half would be married.

With the building of Longview, the opportunity of well paying jobs and a stable work environment would bring many potential employees to the area. The Northwest, at the time of Longview's development, was populated primarily by Scandinavians, with Swedish, Norwegian, Danish and Finnish prominent in the labor force. Climate and opportunity were the attraction to most as it reminded them of their home country. The building of Longview and Ryderwood operations were well advertised in national magazines such as Liberty, Saturday Evening Post and others; the advertising paid off as people poured into the area looking for stable employment One national force normally ignored or overlooked, was the Japanese, who were recruited to work the green chains. A sizeable force of 35 to 40 were employed at Long-Bell and worked on a contract to keep the green chain clean. This proved quite successful and they remained a cohesive unit until the start of World War II, when they and their families were interned during the war.

In developing the information and final report for Long-Bell's management, the engineers had to consider that they knew little about the Northwest. Climate, competition, logging practices, railway connections, Columbia River capabilities and timber availability were all reviewed. Mr. Vandercook , concluded that total available timber in the Northwest was about 940 billion feet, including Washington, Oregon, Idaho and Montana. The area they were most concerned about, Southwest Washington, had approximately 59 billion feet of available timber. Timber type fit three major categories, Douglas Fir, (Oregon Pine) 80%, Hemlock 11% and Western Red Cedar 4% with the balance identified as dead timber. (3)

Logging practices in the Northwest drew considerable comment in the report. The review compared the low elevation, relatively flat terrain in the South, with the rugged areas of the Northwest. Repeated concerns throughout this portion of the study stressed the need for engineering work prior to logging. Comments on the relative ease of laying out roads in the woods in the South, compared with the formidable task of doing the same in the West were of concern. Logging costs would be much higher in the West and the time element needed to prepare an area for logging would be much longer. (4)

The tract of timber purchased by Long-Bell was by examination, of excellent potential. Timber appraisal indicated that grading out the tract consisted of 35% #1, 45% #2 and

20% #3 saw log's, compared to 20% #1, 70% #2, and10% #3 saw logs in the surrounding forest land. With the admonition that it would be expensive to log, it would still be a profitable proposition. (5)

When compared in general terms, logging in the Northwest was not much different than in the South. However with the timber tract in question, the need for extensive engineering was stressed time and again. Past logging practices were often inefficient and wasteful; but accepted, due to timber that was easily accessed. Those tracts were now gone and care was needed to keep cost under control. The use of spar trees and extensive cable systems were the major change from Southern logging practices.

The original report raised a concern about the waste in logging operations of the Northwest. Due primarily to the large diameter of some of the logs during logging operations in the late 1890;s and early 1900's, it was often expedient to leave the largest in the woods. Logs below 18" were felled first as a bed for the larger trees as breakage often occurred when felled. Defective logs were also left in the woods.

Sawmill waste was also considered a massive problem, with only 50% of the log converted into lumber. Bark, sawdust, (wide kerfed saws), slabs and low grade lumber from the interior of the log contributed to the waste. The lumber industry of the teens and 20's was not equipped to convert waste into profitable by-products. There were generally three outlets for the waste; local fuel needs, power generation and the waste burner. Pulp mills were new to the scene and often used cloth rags as a raw material. One of the key considerations for Long-Bell was the development of a power plant to use large quantities of waste wood. Lath mills were also added to the planning process, as a way to decrease waste and increase the savings that would otherwise be burned. (6)

With product waste calculated at 50% of the timber cut, mills were faced with a serious dilemma. Leaving unsound timber in the forest, raised the logging cost substantially, but bringing everything possible to the mill site raised the waste level extremely high. A sample of competing mills in the Northwest indicated major producers were selling their waste wood products to electrical power generators. However, most mills had waste burners operating also. Beginning in the mid 20's, pulp production facilities were being built, offering an outlet for a large portion of the waste developed. Long-Bell would enter into a contract with Crown Willamette (later Crown Zellerbach) for wood waste that was towed to Camas, Washington and West Linn and Oregon City, Oregon for conversion to pulp. (7)

Identifying the mill site was methodical and many locations were reviewed and considered and selecting the site at the confluence of the Cowlitz/Columbia Rivers made the most sense, as it combined the export and domestic transportation opportunities. At one time, sites for a water mill and a separate site for a domestic mill were considered. The Astoria area sites investigated were good for export shipping; but had only one rail line. The Portland/ Haydon Island site had ample rail capability; but was considered marginal for ocean shipping. In both cases logs would need to be transported long distances from the timber stand.

Long-Bell obviously embraced the report and considered all the points identified, when selecting the site and building the mill. That the report was as detailed as it was thorough in scope, speaks well of Long-Bell management. It is highly unlikely that many capital plans during this time period would have been so exacting. Long-Bell management was truly of the top organizations in the industry at this time.

Resource Material :

Engineers Report, The Long-Bell Lumber Company Western Operations, December 10,1920

(1) Pages 10/24

(2) Pages 68/70

(3) Pages 42/44

(4) Pages 71/86

(5) Pages 47

(6) Pages 101/104

(7) Pages 104

Three Long-Bell Douglas Fir trees, containing 50,000 feet log scale. An idea of their great size may be had from observing the man standing between the two trees on the right

Chapter 12

WESTERN OPERATIONS

As the Southern operations reached maturity and Long-Bell purchased a controlling interest in Weed Lumber Company, Weed, California, R. A. Long began to consider the future of his company. Many efforts had been made to acquire additional timberland for the southern mills, with little success. Additional timber had been acquired for Rapidies Lumber Company in central Louisiana, 4000 acres of hardwoods adjacent to Pine Bluff, Arkansas and additional timberlands acquired at Doucette, Texas. A new purchase of a mill at Quitman, Mississippi rounded out their ability to extend the life of the southern operations. Numerous properties were reviewed but in most cases, the timber was too scattered, logging would have been too expensive or the price was too high for a profitable operation.

Long-Bell Log 1975 Vaughan Operations

R. A. Long brought up consideration of investigating western properties in April, 1917 at a board of directors meeting. (1) He suggested forming a search committee to investigate blocking up western timber as the life of southern operations had ten years or less of timber to be cut. The 1920 annual report lists the mills and their expected life: (2)

Calcasieu and Longville	5.4 years	Hudson River	7.4 years
King- Ryder	4.7 Years	Ludington	5.6 years
Lufkin	4.0 years	Doucette	5.9 years
Rapidies	4.6 years	Pine Bluff	2.0 years
Quitman	13.1 years		

The estimates proved to be quite accurate, with the exception of Lufkin, Texas which closed in 1930, Doucette, Texas in 1945 and Quitman, Mississippi which operated until sold in 1963. Obviously timber purchases were made to extend the viability of these operations.

R. A. Long having dealt extensively with Mr. A. H. Cox, General Manager of Weed Lumber Company placed considerable weight on his counsel concerning western timber properties. In the course of this relationship, he became acquainted with R. A. Booth of The Booth- Kelly Lumber Company located in Western Oregon and would rely heavily on these two individuals to filter opportunities for purchasing western timberlands. By 1919 Long-Bell was actively considering timber acquisitions. An option was taken on a tract of timber from The Western Pacific Timber Company located in Southwestern Washington, which was reported to contain 800 million feet of timber on 41,485 acres, at a cost of $1.5 million dollars. The timber was located adjacent to a large block of Weyerhaeuser timber, which Long-Bell also had an interest. The timber on option was in the process of being evaluated. (3)

During the investigation of where to build the western mills, the company received several opportunities to acquire mill properties from existing operators. One of these was Westport Lumber Company, Westport, Oregon. It was investigated and found suitable by S. M. Morris and Mr. Huffman, construction Manager of the Longview plant. An offer was made to acquire the mill but the matter was never finalized. Earlier in 1922, while R. A. Long was in Southern California, Hammond Lumber Company management approached R. A. Long concerning a sale of their properties at Astoria and Garibaldi, Oregon and a Logging operation at Kelso, Washington. At that particular time, Long-Bell was deeply involved with developing the Longview property and passed on the opportunity. (4)

In 1920, Long-Bell purchased approximately 60,000 acres of prime timberland, located in

Southwest Washington, encompassing portions of Cowlitz, Lewis and Wahkiakum counties. The purchase, from Weyerhaeuser consisted of approximately six billion feet of timber, described as 85% Douglas Fir, 10% Hemlock and 5% Western Red Cedar. The volume of timber would be about 100,000 feet per acre, compared to Southern Pine operations of 12,000 to 15,000 feet per acre.

In 1928, Long-Bell purchased a second tract of timber from Weyerhaeuser, adjacent to the original Ryderwood timber purchase. The tract consisted of 57,015 acres, plus cutting rights on 1510 acres of timber. The purchase would be short lived as it was returned to Weyerhaeuser during Long-Bell's struggle to stay solvent during the 1930's. This tract of timber would be known as The MacDonald portion of Weyerhaeuser's Vail-MacDonald Tree Farm. (5)

The original plan for the new facility called for two sawmills with a combined capacity of 900,000 feet for an eight hour day, six days a week. Annual production was rated at 250 million board feet but the mills could exceed the planned volume due to a two shift operation soon after startup. The mills also exceeded their projected cut with ease. When the plan to move west was conceived, the operation was to have the two Mill units (1600 men), Woods operation (900 men), Treating Plant (150 men), Box Factory (300 men), Door Plant (500 men), Sash Plant (300 men), Plywood Plant (100 men) and a Shingle Mill (100 men) for an estimated total employment of 4000 employees. Due to the resulting depression of the 1930's, the Box Plant, Sash and Door plants were not built and the Plywood Plant was acquired from M & M Plywood Companyin 1955.

The two units were to be the largest in the world, at least until Weyerhaeuser built their mills at Longview, Washington, Klamath Falls, Oregon and Lewiston, Idaho. Each of the Long-Bell mills were to be stand alone units, with fairly identical features with the exception that the West mill would include a Factory which produced industrial wood parts, window and door parts, cabinet units and wooden lawn furniture. The West mill began building in 1923 and started up April 1924 and the East mill being built starting in 1924 and started up May 1926.With strong lumber markets, Long-Bell quickly added second shifts to the sawmills, bringing the daily operating volume up to 1,800,000 to 2,000,000 board feet a day. Annual production at Longview, from 1926 through 1929 averaged 318 million board feet a year with 1928 recording production of 427,500,000 board feet.

The West Mill was designed to cut all Douglas Fir, 30" and larger. The mill had 3 head rig's, a 10 foot double cut band saw, a 11 foot single cut band saw and a 7 foot double cut saw, with a length capacity to cut up to 80 feet long. Logs up to 12' in diameter could be sawn; but with difficulty. Anything larger would need to be split in two, usually with dynamite. The West mill band saws were electrically powered, while the East mill had 4 band saws powered by steam. The log carriages in both mills had men riding them in order to set the dogs (clamps holding the logs) and moving the carriage to designed cut width. Sawyers using hand signals indicated the width of the cut. (6)

The East mill cutting 30" diameter and under, cut for actual lumber sizes more frequently than the West mill. The East mill also cut Hemlock and Cedar. Small timbers were cut and cants cut for the gang saw but most of the production went from head saw to trimmer and on to the sorting table. The West mill was considered a breakdown mill, as the log diameter was so large, that the head saws cut timbers, cants and flitches which would be remanufactured farther back in the mill. The West mill thrived on export orders, as it had the capacity to saw items few mills could handle. Timbers 38"x 38" 80 feet long were handled with ease.

A scene from the Long-Bell film, "Lumbering in the Pacific Northwest," showing a loadin
action in the Long-Bell timber near Longview, Wn.

Everything at Longview was big, when it came to processing lumber. The Bull Edger, which was one of the prime breakdown saws and could process a cant 14" thick by 36'inches wide.

Trim saws were designed to cut up to 50 foot long and slasher saws would cut edgings and slabs to 4',4'6" and 5' for the lath mill. The re- manufacturing operation in the back of the mill was designed to process the product of the head saw. Band mill re-saws were smaller in size than the head saws; but were faster and more adaptable to convert the cant or flitch into rough lumber.

An innovation to the Longview mill's, was the drop sorter. Most West Coast mills sent all the rough lumber to the green chain for sorting. At Longview, the East mill was equipped with a 2" drop Sorter, where all 2" lumber moved along a chain, up an incline, where individual pieces would drop out by length on to a table, where it would be sorted by width and heart or sapwood, due to different drying schedules. The lumber would be hand stacked for kiln drying, with separators laid between each layer. The West mill had two Drop Sorters, one for 1" and one for 2". This was due to the large volume of clear lumber being directed toward flooring, ceiling, siding and finish items. (7) All the other items that did not fit these categories went to the green chain. Prior to World War II, Longview green chain's, were manned by a crew of Japanese. Seldom was there lumber that would have to be pulled at the end of the chain and sent back, to be pulled into the proper bin. The Japanese lived in a community adjacent to the West mill shipping sheds, with approximately 38 being employed by Long-Bell.

Lumber pulled on the green chain was moved by overhead monorail crane to an industrial railroad, which moved the lumber to the stacking shed. The railroad consisted of about 30 miles of track and served both green chains. Sixty four dry kilns processed the sawn lumber with forty kilns at the West mill and twenty four at the East mill. With the East mill producing primarily dimension lumber the dry kilns could keep up with the cut, as the moisture content of dry dimension was not as low as clear items resulting in shorter drying schedules.

There was little air drying at West Coast, as early mills were shipping by water. Kiln drying was very important in reducing the weight of lumber products, as most of it was shipped by rail to the Midwest and Eastern markets. Kiln dried lumber would weigh about one third less than green, resulting a much lower freight bill.

The two planer mills could each process 500,000 feet a shift, The West planer had 13 planers and matchers, processing large quantities of flooring, sidings, finish and factory items, while the East planer processed mainly dimension, boards and small posts and timbers with 12 matchers and planers. Both shipping departments combined had the capacity to load 50 cars a day. Car loading, was done on a contract basis, being paid on a per thousand foot rate divided between the two loaders. (8)

The Longview operation became the largest volume producer on the West Coast, until the

Weyerhaeuser mill, also in Longview, reached capacity in 1930. With the exception of the depression years, Longview would be a top producer among West Coast mills until the late 1940's, when raw material constraints limited the production volume.

In addition to the sawmills Longview operations had a lath mill at each head mill. Located beneath each mill, they were incorporated into the conveyer system, which transferred the waste and chip material from the saws. Slabs were cut into 4', 4'6" and 5' lengths by the slasher saws and ripped into 2" wide and 5/16" and ½" thickness. Up to the end of World War II, home construction used plaster as interior wall covering. After that period, Gypsum wallboard captured the market. Plaster was applied to the lath and usually painted after it had dried. The ½" thick lath was used for snow fence, being placed along roadways or rail tracks to hold the snow from blowing. Long-Bell would ship 50/55 million pieces of lath each year, until the mills reduced production. A car load of lath (kiln dried) usually contained 100,000 pieces. (9)

The Longview mill also contained a Shingle mill, which was located on a barge on the log pond, adjacent to the East sawmill, cutting 100,000 shingles a day. The mill operated until the mid 1930's when it was closed, mainly due to continued labor unrest by the Shingle Weavers Union. A Treating Plant was opened in 1947, treating primarily telephone poles, timbers and piling. It operated until 1979/1980. A Particle Board/ Hardboard mill operated on the plant site from 1952 until the early 1960's. The factory operation was an integral part of the West Planer mill, utilizing short length clear lumber. A battery of saws cut lumber for industrial wood parts, cabinets, lawn furniture and many other end uses. Window and door parts were also produced, being shipped in knockdown form to retail yards and the glazing plant at Ft. Smith, Arkansas. The factory was a major supplier of Sears and Roebuck line of Kitchen Cabinets as well as a line of Long-Bell cabinets. Shipments averaged one to one and a half million feet a month, with carloads containing 80,000 feet of lumber with up to 70,000 pieces in a car. The factory ran as a separate entity employing 150 or more employees. (10)

Ryderwood Loggers 1928

Long-Bell knew that the timber supply for the Longview complex was diminishing quickly and by the end of 1953, it was time to begin the curtailment of the operation. The East mill complex sawed the last log at the end of January 1954. The West mill expanded to two shifts; but it could also see the end. On May 13, 1960, the last log was cut, ending 36 years of production. The West mill cut 4,475,000,000 feet of lumber and the East mill cut 4,210,000,000 feet of lumber, for a grand total of 8,655 billion feet.

Despite their troubles during the depression years, the Longview operations re-bounded in the late 1930's and with the war years shipped 25% of the total production during this period. In 1941, the two mills shipped 518 million feet, of which 60 million was purchased from other sources. (11) Long-Bell consistently purchased rough green lumber from small local mills, melding the production in with its own. This was done to utilize the existing units, such as the dry kilns and planer mills. 2"x 4"8 foot long, rough lumber was purchased in large volume, as it was not economical to produce it in these huge mills. With the building boom of the post war years, this item was in great demand.

Long-Bell was able to generate sufficient earnings to satisfy their court- mandated obligations by 1942. With wartime demand and satisfactory prices, the company was able to set aside funds for future expansion. In June 1945, the company purchased Snellstrom Lumber Company, Vaughan, Oregon, approximately 18 miles West of Eugene, Oregon. The mill consisted of a sawmill, planer and a short line railroad, which connected to the Southern Pacific railroad. The purchase also included 39,000 acres of timberland. The sawmill had a capacity of 25 to30 million board feet of lumber per year.(12). On July 30th, 1949 the Vaughan sawmill was destroyed by fire, rebuilt and restarted in 1950 with production increased to 30 million board feet. A new planer was added in 1952, and a Plywood plant in 1956, with a capacity of 50 million feet on a 3/8 basis, employing 250. Continued investment in the Vaughan operation occurred in 1960 by modernizing the sawmill and plywood plants. The sawmill increased capacity to 200,000 thousand feet a shift and employing 650 employees. Timberland also grew to 77,000 acres.

In 1947, Long-Bell acquired the Austa Lumber Company, adjacent to the Vaughan operation, cutting 60,000 feet a day or about 13 million board feet a year. The mill operated until about 1956 when Long-Bell was merged with International Paper. The two mills were managed as one unit, with George Hays, long time company employee as manager. (13)

In April 1948, Long-Bell acquired two sawmills from the Gardiner Lumber Company, Gardiner, Oregon, for $ 5 million dollars. The two mills produced 92 million board feet in 1947 with 400 employees. Sixty percent of the volume was shipped by inter-coastal vessels primarily to California ports. Timberlands of 75,000 acres were included in the purchase. The timber abuts the Vaughan holdings of Long-Bell. At the time of the purchase, the Bridge mill in Reedsport, Oregon had rail access connecting to the Southern Pacific railroad. The Gardiner mill was strictly water shipment until 1950 when a rail spur connected the mill to the Southern Pacific. (14) At that time, the company built a 60 million feet 3/8 basis plywood plant and converted the sawmill to a mixed car mill with dry kilns, a new planer mill, dry storage sheds and rail car loading facilities for loading 8 cars a day. This was completed in 1953. By 1954 further improvements were made, increasing loading capacity to 13 cars a day. In 1963 International Paper Company remodeled the sawmill utilizing the latest equipment, specializing in dimension lumber, some industrial clears and export clears. Daily capacity was 125,000 feet, on a one shift basis. Also incorporated into the plant site was a small log mill cutting peeler cores and small logs into 2"x4" 8 foot lumber with a 25,000 foot per shift capacity.

In the late 1970's, International Paper had totally re-built the Gardiner sawmill, putting in a highly automated mill cutting small logs at a cost of $77 million dollars. It only ran for a short period of time before it was closed due to market conditions. The Gardiner operation had two very serious forest fires, Vincent Creek and the Oxbow fire in the upper Smith River timberlands, which seriously limited the life of the Gardiner operation.

SINGLE CRANE sweeps above stacks of lumber packages in expediting production flow in Chelatchie's lumber handling shed. Storage capacity of the 800-foot-long and 112-foot-wide structure is 4½ million board feet.

In 1953 Long-Bell looking to extend their operations, purchased the Oregon American mill at Vernonia, Oregon operation from Central Coal and Coke Company. The mill with a capacity of 60 million board feet per year was built in 1926 and included 20,000 acres of timberland. The mill was a mixed car mill and was of all steel construction. Oregon American had a difficult existence having been through bankruptcy, closed for about three years during the depression and suffered severe loss of timber during the numerous Tillamook Burn fires of the 1930's and 1940's. At the peak of its operations in 1928, it cut 161 million feet. The mill site at Vernonia, Oregon was limited on labor supply due to its remote location. Central Coal and Coke, the parent company was forced to import Filipino's, Greeks, Hindu and Blacks to augment their crew. The Blacks came from Central Coal and Coke's lumber operations at Conroe, Texas. Each group lived in their own small segregated community. (15)

While it is not clear why Long-Bell purchased the Vernonia mill, due to its limited timber supply, it did provide three years of production and added the 20,000 acres to the Long-Bell Tree Farm system, which would be needed for the future. The mill closed in July 1957.

In 1956 Long-Bell merged with International Paper Company and still had some life left as a lumber producer. While the Longview operation was still viable, Long-Bell had numerous dealings with Harbor Plywood, Hoquiam, Washington, on a large tract of timber located in Eastern Clark County, Washington on the upper North Fork of the Lewis River. The timber known as the Peterman tract was the result of a purchase of cutting rights from the Northern Pacific railroad and plans had been made to build conversion facilities in the Chelatchie Prairie/Amboy area of Clark County. The Northern Pacific agreement insisted that facilities be built, which would use their railroad line for transportation.

Harbor Plywood purchased the cutting rights for the timber from the Peterman family and began logging up to 90 million feet ahead of the establishment of production facilities. This was done to generate cash flow, which enabled Harbor to begin building the logging road needed to tap the timber. The road was 20 miles long, which went from Chelatchie Prairie to Pine Creek on the upper Lewis River. Long-Bell made a $ 1 million dollar no interest loan to help pay for the road. This was done to allow Long-Bell the opportunity to purchase saw logs developing from the logging and intended for the Longview mill. (16)

Harbor Plywood was a corporation originally based in Chicago, Illinois and while there is little evidence that Long-Bell had any financial investment other than the loan, Roy Morse, Long-Bell's land and timber manager was on the Plywood company board of directors. Detailed plans were made to erect a sawmill, plywood plant, a shingle mill and sash and door plants at Chelatchie Prairie by Harbor Plywood. A plat for a town and test driving of piling was accomplished in 1948.

The entire complex was to cost an estimated $42 million dollars. In 1950 Long-Bell and Harbor Plywood entered into a contract for purchasing saw logs from the Peterman Tract, however in 1955 Harbor Plywood sued Long-Bell, in an effort to rescind the agreement, asking $35 million dollars in damages. The suit was settled in the late 1950's, with Long-Bell paying $2 million dollars to Harbor Plywood and Long-Bell acquiring the Peterman cutting rights on the remaining timber. Access to this timber also opened the way for Forest Service timber sales to augment the timber supply. (17)

In 1959 construction of a sawmill and Plywood plant had begun, with a startup date scheduled for mid 1960. The Plywood plant had a capacity of 72 million feet, 3/8 basis and sawmill was rated at 42 million board feet annually. The latest innovative equipment was installed and the Plywood plant had steam vaults for peeler block steaming, a new innovation as well as pre spotting blocks for the lathe. Both innovations increased recovery and allowed for reduced roundup at the lathe. The Plywood plant produced Hardwood plywood in addition to Douglas Fir items. Birch and Mahogany face grade was imported and combined with Douglas Fir to make the panel. This quality panel added revenue well over that of the Fir panel. The new facility employed 250 at the plywood plant and 150 in the sawmill and 150 loggers.(18) Chelatchie Prairie operated from 1960 until 1979 and in that time period, well over one and a half billion feet of timber was cut from the Peterman tract and Forest Service timber sales. In contrast to the Longview operation, housing was not provided for the employees. The community's of Amboy and Yacolt absorbed many families; but the bulk of them commuted from Longview and Vancouver, WA. In the 19 years of operation, the Plywood plant produced 1.6 billion feet 3/8 basis and sawmill produced approximately 824,638,000 board feet of lumber.

The years from 1924 through 1980, Long-Bell/ International Paper produced 12, 366 billion feet of lumber products at Western mills, plus unknown purchases of green and dry lumber. An amazing achievement for a leading producer of softwood lumber

Once the initial purchase was made, preparations were made to establish the logging operation in Northern Cowlitz County, near Vader, WA. The company planned to develop a town site called Ryderwood, (named after W. F. Ryder, a long time Long-Bell associate) which would be the woods headquarters. A work force of up to 900 loggers, railroad and maintenance workers was envisioned. As with the mill site at Longview, a town would need to be built to house the workers and their families. This was to be one of the first family camps in the Northwest. (19)

With the mountainous terrain to be logged, a major project to develop a topographical map and model was undertaken, in order to generate the Lowe'st logging costs possible. The relief map built in sections, covered every detail of the terrain to be logged. When finished, it measured 30'x 40' and proved to be invaluable to the woods engineers and logging managers over the life of the operation. Long-Bell was not reluctant to spend money where they thought the return was worth it.

With Long-Bell's experience at Weed, California operations and their extensive exposure to West Coast lumber products through the Tacoma/ Seattle purchasing office, the company would have some knowledge of the Western timber and logging practices. However, company management had little exposure to the complexities in Douglas Fir forests. In 1918, when it was decided to continue the company's operations with a move west, very little was known about the forested region by company officials. Only after the timber stand had been identified and viewed, did management begin to comprehend what was needed to enter into logging Douglas Fir forests.

Also the companies experience with Southern and Weed logging related to family connections rather than the itinerant logger of the Northwest. Provision must be made for family quarters in order to attract the best workers.

With the topographical survey completed, preparations were under way to build the housing for the workers, start the logging railroad into the woods and build a connection via rail to Longview and the mill site. The town of Ryderwood was to be a first in the Northwest as loggers usually lived in remote camps far from civilization. One of the reasons that loggers were so quick to move on, was the conditions that existed in the camps. Poor food would clear out a camp quickly. Sleeping quarters were crowded and often insect infested. Long-Bell was used to camps close by and strived to maintain a stable labor force. The company was reported to pay higher wages for stability and labor peace.

Building the town site required that detailed planning be done in order to separate the commercial areas from residential and family housing from the rooming houses. Ryderwood, had schools, a community hall, theatre, restaurant/ tavern, boarding houses and a town constable to keep the peace. By 1923, 75 houses had been built and in 1924 100 more had been added and a connection had been made with the main line of the railroad. The ability to move trainloads of logs to the mill at Longview was a reality in little over a year. In this time a town had been formed, 5.7 miles of rail to the main line, 25 miles of woods railroad, 10 locomotives had been delivered and water and electricity connections completed.(20)

On June 18, 1924, the first logs moved from the woods to Longview and the daily process of moving logs to the mill started. The delivery of logs by train would continue until the late 1940's on a two trains per day basis. Initially logs moved from Ryderwood to the main line of the railroad (Northern Pacific, Great Northern and Union Pacific) at Vader, Washington then to Longview Junction. Eventually the Longview, Portland and Northern Railroad (a Long-Bell subsidiary) would operate on a route west of the Cowlitz River, from Ryderwood to Longview. This route was used until

1933, when a disastrous flood wiped out several sections of the track. The line was not rebuilt and the transfer reverted to the main line.

One of the many innovations Long-Bell employed in developing the logging operations was to extend electrical lines from the mill to the woods operation. This was highly unusual as the typical woods landing was steam donkey or skidder. Another example of Long-Bell's willingness to spend money if they felt the return was worth it. Long-Bell was an innovator in many respects and the logging world was introduced to electricity mainly through them. In the early 1920's, a few logging companies had tried the use of electrical power for yarding and loading of logs but Long-Bell was the first to incorporate the entire operation to electrical use. (21)

Through use of wood refuse and hogged fuel, power was generated to operate the mills, town and woods operation. The powerhouse generated 24,000 kilowatts per day. From a sub- station north of Longview, Washington, the transmission line ran 32 miles to the Ryderwood, Washington Sub-station. From this location, it was broken down to 13,000 volts of electricity. The feeder lines from Ryderwood, went through the woods to portable sub-stations, reduced further to down to 600 volts, reducing costs by 25/35%. When a sub-station moved, the line feeding it followed or extended as the move required.

The company's electrical logging operation had 12 sub-stations and the transformers were fastened to fourteen foot log skids, connected by six cross members, so that the sub-station could be easily moved. A steam crane loads and unloads the sub-station when required. The cables running from the sub-station were wrapped in waterproof tape as they were often buried or exposed to moisture. In the mid 1920's, the company operated 10 logging sides equipped with electrical skidding capability. Six car mounted combination yarder/loader, a two car mounted interlocking skidder and loader and seven single yarders mounted on skids. Despite the obstacles woods electrical operations might possess, the company was extremely happy with the results.

The equipment used at Ryderwood was produced by Washington Iron Works, Seattle, Washington and Willamette Iron and Steel, Portland, Oregon, who were well known equipment manufacturers and suppliers. Each company supplied three combination yarders and loaders, one combination skidder and loader and one single sled mounted yarder. There was very little difference between the two companies, with Willamette units employing a gearing device which was controlled and shifted by compressed air to obtain high and low speeds on main the yarding lines, while the Washington units employ a single two speed motor to obtain the desired line speed. The skidders cost $50,000 each and the loaders $35,000 each. A steam (wood burning) skidder/loader would have been much less, while a new Diesel skidder cost about $115,000. This Diesel skidder was the first ever built. The cost of a steam Donkey Engine is not known; but it would fall into the range of $15/20,000. (22)

By the late 1920's, Long-Bell had excellent cost control of their logging operations. The electric units cost $20.00 per day, steam $12.00 and diesel$3.00 per day, with the average logging side loading 150,000fbm per day. The operating costs from a logging side were about $65.00 a day (early 30's) or 30 cents per m steam, 12 cents for electricity and 3 cents for diesel. By 1928 the company was operating 22 sides at Ryderwood, 10 electric, 12 steam and one diesel. Eight hundred men were employed, with over 50 miles of spur track. Over 1million feet of logs were moved to the mill daily. (23)

A logging side was consisted of the following personnel. Two sets of fallers, one bucker and a scaler who scales for five sets of fallers. The fallers and buckers work on a contract basis, with fallers receiving 16.5 cents per m each and the bucker 26.5 cents per m (1933 wage scale), the scaler receives $6.00 per day. Not much money for back breaking work but good for the depression era. Fallers would cut about 40m per day and the buckers cutting about 30 m. Buckers cut logs from 16' to 68 'lengths and scale was based on Columbia River Log Scale. (24)

Logs were brought to the landing by two major systems, "tight skyline", operated by the steam and diesel skidders and the "high lead systems" operated by the electrical units. Specially designed yarders were also operated to bring in logs from inaccessible places, saving the cost of building spurs. The crewing of the skidding and loading operation (1935) was skidder foreman @$9.00 per day, second rigger@$7.00 (in charge of rigging crew), hooker (picks out logs to be loaded and signals whistle punk) $6.00 a day, powder monkey@ $4.75, 4 choker setters $4.75, one hook chaser $4.75, skidding engineer @ $7.50, loading engineer @ $6.50, head loader @ $7.00 and tong chasers @ $4.75. The crew was expected to load 150,000 feet a day. Logs were loaded on specially built log cars, holding approximately 12,000 feet of logs. A train of approximately 80 cars was sent to the mill, with two trains a day the norm.

With the depression of the 1930's, logging and mill operations were severely curtailed. Logging was reduced to about half the normal rate of production With the inception of the Lumber Code Authority in 1934 Long-Bell was limited to 900,000 feet of logs per day. Logging was reduced to six sides from a high of twenty two, with each side limited to 150,000 feet. (25)

By the late 1930's, having gone through a major re-organization, Long-Bell needed to change how they operated their timber department and also to find more timber in order to keep the mills operating at capacity. In 1937 the company began to contract some of their logging sites at Ryderwood. The depression reduced employment from a high of 900 employees down to 400 to 500 by the late 1930's. Atlas Logging had a close tie to Long-Bell and they were awarded a contract to log

36 million feet of timber. By the time Atlas Logging completed logging in the Ryderwood area, the volume would be in the hundreds of millions feet.

The company was continually looking for additional timberlands to support the Longview mills. In January 1938, the company purchased a tract of timber at Cochran, Oregon, located at the headwaters of the Salmonberry River deep in the Tillamook forest. The timber at Cochran was in scattered pockets, left over from the 1933 Tillamook Fire and very difficult to log. Long-Bell logged this tract of timber until 1947, when Atlas Logging took over the site.

Here is the sight which greeted Ed Itor as the "Spirit of Long-Bell" hovered over the Longview, Wn., plants. The buildings on the left are the West Fir unit, the power plant (with the two tall smokestacks) is just left of the center of the picture and the East Fir unit is on the right

Long-Bell Log Longview Plant SiteFebruary 1928

Atlas purchased the logging camp and equipment and converted it into a truck operation. The railroad was torn up, with some rails going to Longview and Vaughan operations and some rails were sent to the Southern Pacific Railroad as replacement for rails furnished to Weed logging operations. Atlas logging pulled many million feet of logs from those narrow canyons and at a much lower cost. Atlas also took on a contract to log 100 million feet of fire killed timber in the Tillamook Burn area that Long-Bell had acquired.

In 1942 Long-Bell acquired title to approximately 19,000 acres of timber land in Polk County, Oregon from the Miami Corporation. Logging was done on a contract basis, with Long-Bell building the roads as this was 100% truck operation. Logs were hauled to Grande Ronde, Oregon, dumped into a log pond for sorting and loaded on rail cars for hauling to Longview mills. The operation had 32 miles of truck roads. Also in 1942 the company acquired attract of timber in the Winston Creek area, south of Kosmos, Washington, close to the site of Mayfield Dam on the Cowlitz River. The logging at this location was also 100 % contract, trucked to East Winston sorted and railed to Longview. There were eleven miles of road, with an additional 25 miles to be added. The operation lasted until the mid 1950's. In 1943 Long-Bell established a log buying station at Sweet Home, Oregon. Logs were purchased from local logging companies, with plywood peelers sold locally and the rest railed to Longview. The operation was closed down in 1950.

With the end of World War I, the need for new housing opened up the opportunity for cutting timber from National Forest lands. Long-Bell took serious advantage of this timber supply by logging extensively in the Carson/Skamania County Washington area. They established a log dump at Wind River, Washington on the upper Columbia River. Forest Service timber sales would be utilized until the Longview and Chelatchie Prairie mills were closed.

In 1947 Long-Bell took a serious look at their timber situation for the Longview operation. At a meeting of the board of directors, August 11, 1947, Roy Morse head of timberlands for the company summarized the situation.

Ryderwood- Has cut (1924 to 7-1-1947) 2,922,716 feet of timber. Left to cut, 336 million feet.

Winston Creek- Has cut (1942 to 7-1-1947) 551,590,002 feet of timber. Left to cut 237 million feet.

Grande Ronde has cut (1943 t0 7-1- 1947) 147,497,940 feet of timber. Left to cut 396 million feet.

Cochran has cut (1942 to 7-1- 1947) 346,165,320 feet of timber. Left to cut 204 million feet, which included 40 million feet of fire killed timber from 1933 Tillamook fire. In addition the company had a contract with Tillamook County to log 100 million feet of fire killed timber owned by the county. Total amount cut 3,978 billion feet of timber and left to cut 1,173 billion feet of timber. Mr. Morse also reported that labor troubles in some areas were bothersome and were looking at a couple small sawmills in the Winston Creek area to cut small timber and haul it to Longview for processing rather than bringing in the logs. (26)

One of the very important factors in Longview's existence was the purchase of logs on the open market. For many years the Columbia River market area furnished logs for many manufacturers. From the very beginning of the mills existence at Longview, the company took full advantage of log availability, purchasing from a variety of suppliers. Hammond Lumber Company had an operation in East Kelso who supplied logs to Long-Bell. Crown Zellerbach was a major supplier from their Cathlamet, Washington operations. Log purchases continued until the Longview operations closed down in 1961.

Reference:

(1)   Long-Bell Board of Director Meeting Notes, April 5, 1917

(2)   Long-Bell Financial Statement, January 1, 1921

(3)   Long-Bell Board of Director Meeting Notes, October 8, 1919

(4)   Long-Bell Board of Director Meeting Notes, November 9, 1922

(5)   Longview Daily News, January 12, 1928, Page 1

(6)   The Timberman Magazine, August 1924, Page 49 & 52

(7)   The Timberman Magazine, August 1924, Page 50

(8)   Long-Bell Log, September 1924, Page 2

(9)   Long-Bell Log, March 1928, Page 9

(10)   Long-Bell Log, March 1928, Page 13

(11)   Forests For The Future, Rodney C. Loehr , Page 224

(12)   Longview Daily News, July 7, 1945, Page 1

(13)   Longview Daily News, June 30, 1947, Page 1

(14)   Longview Daily News, April 4, 1948, Page 1

(15)   Oregon American Lumber Company Ain't No More Edward J. Kamholz, Jim Bain & Gary Kamholz, Page 298

(16)   The Story of Frank D. Hobi, Margret Elly Felt, Page 130

(17)   Longview Daily News, March 3, 1948 , Page 1

(18)   Long-Bell Log, May 1961, Page 10

(19)   Long-Bell Log, May 1928, Page 6 & 7

(20)   Long-Bell Log, May 1928, Page 5

(21)   Long-Bell Log, July 1925, Page 15 to17

(22)   Internal Long-Bell Document, 1934 Page 5

(23)   Internal Long-Bell Document, 1934   Page 7

(24)	Internal Long-Bell Document, 1934, Page 3 & 4

(25)	Internal Long-Bell Document , 1934, Page 2

(26)	Roy F. Morse Board of Directors Presentation, August 11, 1947

Scenes From The Long-Bell Manufacturing Plants at Longview

Some views photographed in and around the Long-Bell Douglas Fir lumber manufacturing plants at Longview, Wash. No. 1 shows the electric power plant as it appears from the Columbia River. Each of the two stacks is 300 feet high, 21 feet inside top diameter, and 30 feet outside bottom diameter. No. 2—An interior view of one of two dry sorters of the unstacker sheds, each of which is 1,228 feet long. No. 3—An end view of log carriage in the head mill. No. 4—End of fuel house showing conveyor chains and motor drives. No. 5—A double-cut band saw in the head mill. No. 6—Two electric bridge cranes on the timber dock.

No. 7—Interior of filing room, showing machines for sharpening the great band saws. No. 8—Shows a part of the drop sorter shed. No. 9—One of 3 electric transfer cars, each with a capacity of 20 tons, which transfer cars of green lumber from the stackers to the dry kilns. In the background is seen a part of the battery of 40 dry kilns, each of which measures 12'x120' inside and each has a capacity of 32,000 board feet. No. 10—Conveyor belt to carry hogged fuel from the mill to the fuel house. No. 11—Conveyor belt that carries hogged fuel from the fuel house to the furnace room. No. 12—A large deck saw in the head mill.

Page 18

Page

Chapter 13

TAKING CARE OF THE FOREST

Reviewing the activities of lumber and logging companies active in the late 19th and early 20th century, one of the last things considered was conservation and re-forestation. Prior to the end of the 19th century, serious agitation was coming from notable national leaders including President Theodore Roosevelt and Gifford Pinchot a leading forest conservationist. There were many individuals engaged in the lumber business, that also expressed concern over forest depletion, but nationally little effort was generated to do anything about the issue.

Throughout the history of the lumber industry, land sales from cut over areas had been attempted. Cheap land was offered to would be farmers throughout the country, with limited results. In the case of Long-Bell, they set up an experimental farm, in Southern Louisiana, to demonstrate that farm crops could be grown. Unfortunately the land offered from the cut over land was seldom suitable to grow anything other than trees.

After the turn of the century, farsighted companies began to be concerned about long term timber supply. The need for revising existing tax laws was a factor in keeping cutover land or disposing of it. One way was to allow the land to revert to the state in lieu of non- payment of taxes. To many operators, this was not the desirable thing to do. Agitation for tax relief began in the early 1900's and gained momentum in the 1920's as the movement toward retaining cut over land reached its peak. Forestland was taxed the same as agricultural land on an annual basis. States, which were heavily timbered, realized that changes needed to be made in severance tax laws in order to keep the land in timber owner's hands. Growing new crops of trees would insure future tax revenue.

Major lumber producers were concerned that continued cut and get out practices had to change. Public pressure on continued cutting of timber without thought for reforestation was mounting. Despite having vast forests potentially at their disposal, the image of the logger cutting wide swaths through the area was one they deplored, efforts toward returning the land to productivity, was needed. As early as 1905, lumber companies were considering methods of re-forestation. In 1911, Henry Hardtner, owner of Urania Lumber Company, Urania, Louisiana, began planting 75,000 acres of Loblolly Pine seedlings on his cut over land.(1) He was one of the first non-foresters to recognize that to stay in business, his company needed to provide for the future. The timberlands planted still provide timber for Louisiana Pacific's Plywood and Oriented Strand board plants today. Other Southern companies involved with re-forestation were, Crossett Lumber Company, located in southern Arkansas, Kaul Lumber Company in Alabama, Dierks Lumber Company of Arkansas and Oklahoma, Great Southern Lumber Company, Bogalusa, Louisiana and Jackson Lumber Company, Lockhart, Alabama. In the early 1900's, there were few foresters available to help with the technical aspects of forest regeneration. The few that had the knowledge were involved with the fledgling United States Forest Service or teaching in the newly established forestry schools. The effort toward re-forestation was initiated from a practical need, as the trained forester had long preached that the forests would run out unless measures were taken to replenish the supply.

It should be established that care of the forestland included control of fire, as well as the growing of trees. Disastrous fires plagued the Pacific Northwest, in 1902, 1910, 1918, 1933, 1939, 1945, and 1951, when millions of timbered acres went up in flames. Agitation for better fire protection and tax relief began in the late teens and early 20's at the state and federal level. Changing the taxation basis to a severance tax was the favored method.

One result of the massive forest fires in the Northwest was the establishment of a Forest Service experiment station at Wind River, Washington in 1909. As early as 1903, Forest Service workers were looking at the results of the Yacolt fire. The Wind River valley was a natural location for study as the southern side of the valley burned, while the north side was untouched. Thurman T. Munger was the first director and the station was dedicated in 1913.

With the Forest Service becoming a new federal agency, personnel was struggling to organize and develop the planning for operating the new bureau. Reforestation while important did not receive the attention it deserved. The newly formed Forest Service was fought at every location by ranchers, sheep men, loggers and politicians. In addition to start up complexities, World War I began and many of the fledgling foresters were called into wartime service, primarily with the Forestry Corp, which operated sawmills in France, cutting timber for use in the battlefields.

By the early 1920's, Long-Bell realized that something had to be done to allow perpetuation of the forests. In 1923 John B. Woods, a professional forester, who had previously been engaged in timber appraisal by the federal government, was hired to analyze Long-Bell timber and cut over land to determine best uses. His first task was to assess each area of cut over land, developing a plan of action for the unit. In his initial studies, ample evidence was available of farms abandoned due soil being too poor for farming. These efforts resulted in the survey of over 200,000 acres in Mississippi, Louisiana, Arkansas, and Texas. (2)

Although actual re-forestation efforts had not begun, the survey and forest engineering advice from John Woods pointed the direction toward thinning, clearing fire trails and developing growth and yield data on the various tracts of timber. In 1925, an experimental planting of Long Leaf Pine was planned. The plantations were at Longville, Louisiana, (800 acres) and De Ridder, Louisiana, two locations of 420 acres total. This was a start toward a continued reforestation effort, except for a pause during the depression. With the uncertainties of taxation, it was not yet possible to see what the future of re-forestation would be. (3)

While studies were being made in the south, a survey of western lands in California and Washington had been completed in 1925 and definite plans were made to establish a tree nursery at Ryderwood, Washington The plan which had a five year duration, called for hand planting seedlings on 3/4000 acres a year. Experiments in direct seeding were also to be conducted. The goal was to replant an area equal to the area logged. One feature of the re-forestation effort was to establish fire lanes of Alder and Maple along abandoned railroad lines which would divide the forest into smaller more manageable units and facilitate protection of the new forests. Snags were felled if they presented a potential fire hazard. Slash disposal methods followed closely the state laws. Company fire patrols were set up to protect cut over lands as well as the virgin forest (4)

In developing the forest plan for the Ryderwood tract, John Woods and his crew, were methodical in their evaluation of the cut over land. Drawing on the original timber cruise they had a breakdown of specie, climate, terrain and accessibility to the areas to be considered for planting. An examination of the soils indicated in most areas that the soil was not suitable for farming and especially the steep slopes where erosion was probable, if farming was attempted. Otherwise soils were ideal for replanting to trees. Developing a plan for reforesting the cut over lands, the planner's did not have any precedent to fall back on, as little had been done toward researching of forest soils. While a daunting task, the foresters took it as a challenge. They looked at the task as a healthy condition and it should be the beginning of commercial forest regeneration. In the planning process, the agreed on two points, that reforested land was desirable and fire prevention is necessary. It was in these deliberations, about the growing of second growth Douglas Fir they found that a new crop could not be raised in the shadow of old growth with any success. From some of the studies information was developed that second growth, stagnated after 30 years unless the stand was thinned to some degree. Every effort was made to investigate and record the best methods to be used in growing a new forest. (5)

The report prepared by John Woods took into consideration land values, yield from second growth timber, taxes on cut over or re-forested land and cost of replanting. He put forth in his report that replanted lands might need to be held for up to 50 years prior to having timber worth cutting. It was pointed out that this certainly would not keep the mills in Longview operating without additional old growth purchases. The report took into consideration natural seeding; but that at least 50% of the land would need hand planting. It was estimated that it would cost $5.00 per acre to plant the cutover ground.

A proposal was put forth to develop the Ryderwood tree nursery within a five year plan. The nursery was to be developed to grow two or three year old seedlings at the rate of 1 million per year. The plan reaching fruition in 1930 would have planted 12,000 acres, which would include some natural seeding. Actual planting was done each year, 1926 through 1929; but was curtailed, then discontinued during the depression. The success of this forward planning would be evident by the 1950's and beyond. Cost estimates were made and presented to management for their approval. For the five year period, a budget of $62,850 in 1925 dollars was forecast as the needed expenditure. (6)

The California lands were also being surveyed, to determine how best to reforest. Logging in Pine timberland was different than the western slopes of the cascades, as timber harvesting was based on selective cutting rather than clear cutting. Pine timber did have more problems with insects and disease such as Blister Rust, which were as troublesome as fire. California had experience with reforestation as Redwood forests had replanted previously with good results. (7) While the Ryderwood and Southern forest approach to reforestation was done on an experimental basis, Long-Bell management felt the results would certainly prove out to be an ongoing venture.

The Long-Bell Plantation, as it appeared shortly before the merger of Long-Bell with International Paper Company in 1956.

With the acceptance of the philosophy that reforestation was the only way a company could stay in business for the long term, Long-Bell management moved ahead on longer term forestry projects. With establishment of the nursery at Ryderwood, growing seedlings of other specie than Douglas Fir were planned. Developing an understanding of what specie would survive in the local climate was important. Efforts were made to grow Redwood, Port Orford Cedar and Ponderosa Pine; but the major efforts were made to grow Douglas Fir, Hemlock and Western Red Cedar. Hand replanting was the method of transferring the seedlings to the ground. Long-Bell did utilize the method of seed trees on the ridge tops to naturally seed all the areas possible, although the foresters were skeptical that seeds would not blow more than 100 yards from the source. While Long-Bell was among the first to consider replanting in the west, considerable work, had been done in reforestation research and the benefits of sustained yield, by David Mason, of Mason and Stevens, consulting foresters located in Portland, Oregon.

Fire prevention was a major segment of the reforestation process. Twenty foot lines were built along abandoned railroad spurs. This method of fire prevention was a new feature, not being used in the west prior to the company developing it at Ryderwood. Foresters in the west and British Columbia watched with interest.

As emphasis on reforestation grew, the need to educate the public was identified. The cut and get out philosophy among the timber companies had cast an unfavorable light on the industry for a long time. Seizing on an opportunity to turn public favor toward their cause, Long-Bell and other timber companies used the media and other venues to inform the public about the advantage of reforestation. Trade publications, service clubs meetings and the formation of boys forestry clubs in Louisiana were all used to spread the message (8) Long-Bell quickened the pace of reforestation, by establishing forest nurseries at De Ridder and Longville, Louisiana. Through collection of seed cones at logging sites, 8,000# of Longleaf and 3,000# of Shortleaf Pine cones were gathered. 3 pounds of clean dry seed were recovered from 100pounds of green cones. It took 9 to10 months from the time seed was planted until it was suitable for re planting. In 1928, Long-Bell intended to reforest 1,000 acres with about 1 million seedlings. The plan called for 900 to 1000 seedlings per acre, considering a 10/15% mortality rate. Thinning would be done in 12 to 15 years, yielding posts, which would be about 50% of the stand. In 5 to 10 year intervals, further thinning would be made. At an age of 35/45 years, 100/125 trees would be left, measuring 20"/25" at the stump. (9)

The 1920's, was the time when private forestry grew up. Recognition throughout the industry that efforts needed to replace forests being cut was required to sustain the long term life of a company. Throughout the nations forested regions, efforts toward reforestation and sustained yield were being discussed and implemented. Weyerhaeuser Timber Company, the nation's largest timber owner, set up a special reforestation company capitalized at $1 million. States were beginning to change their taxation and fire protection laws and many of the major southern lumber companies implemented reforestation efforts. Urania Lumber Company, which pioneered reforestation efforts in 1905, was beginning to cut the new forest.

This is the reforestation plot of Joe Jones, youngest son of William Jones, field man for the Long-Bell Creosoting Division at Shreveport, La. It is near Noble, La., on land that was a log pond prior to 1916. Joe is on the extreme left near the sign

Coupled with the movement to reforest the land, efforts were being made to utilize the byproducts. Southern Lumber Company, Bogalousa, Louisiana replaced its refuse burner with a pulp mill. Weyerhaeuser Timber Company began to develop pulp facilities in Minnesota, as well as a wood conversion company to produce Balsa Wool from former weed trees while other companies developed box plants to utilize short length lumber.

The regeneration of cutover land, suffered a serious blow during the long depression of the 1930's. Funds allocated toward nursery stock and replanting disappeared. The fight for survival cut many corners; but the effort toward reforestation would remain. National attention through Keep Oregon and Washington Green programs and similar efforts in other states would keep the emphasis growing. Civilian Conservation Corps programs developed during the depression would aid reforestation efforts through road building, soil erosion control, snag cutting for fire protection in burned areas and tree planting in federal forests. The nation felt strongly enough about reforestation, that provisions were inserted into the National Lumber Code, developed as a means to even out the available business among all producers.

Federal forestry officials and conservationists had long pushed for tighter control of logging in the nation's forests, fearing that the supply of timber would be depleted quickly. Many mill operators had the same feeling; but were handicapped in changing their ways without a change in the tax code. Even though Long-Bell, Weyerhaeuser and others had taken steps to extend the life of their companies through re-forestation and fire control, the skeptics were many. (10) As part of the National Recovery Act, conservation of timber resources and tax revision were included in the act. Sustained yield of forest resources was to be the national goal, covering all 500 million acres of federal, state, private and other holdings of timberland.

With the reduced need for lumber products due to the depression, the lumber code authority was deemed the proper method for addressing the control of forest depletion. Article X of the recovery act laid out logging practices, reforestation methods, and instructions to insure sufficient seed trees were left to adequately reseed the new forest. Although the lumber code authority did not survive, the forestry section continued to function. The forest fire prevention and tax relief sections of the code were enacted, giving hope to the sustainability of private forests in the future. Fire prevention and suitable tax laws were enacted in many states to sustain holding of timber for long periods. Weyerhaeuser's dedication of their Southwest Washington Tree Farm in 1941 started a national movement towards protecting timber stands large and small. The emphasis was there to put forest protection on a solid footing. Today we reap the benefits, as our timber supply comes from private stands in the second, third or even fourth cuttings.

The 1930- 1939 depression halted any thought of continuing reforestation for Long-Bell. Filing for bankruptcy, little business opportunity and coping with the company efforts to recover, left nothing available for the re-planting of trees. John Woods, chief forester left the company and joined the West Coast Lumbermen Association. However the idea of regeneration for future timber crops never left the company's management plan. With available timberland in short supply, other than national forest land, replanting of their timberland had to be a top priority.

With Long-Bell, implementing its reforestation efforts, in the mid 20's, the planting began modestly, more of an experiment than a long term plan. However as results began to show benefits, management increased their commitment to recover the logged off land. By 1931, the state of Washington had passed a timber tax act stating taxes will be lowered on land that had been reforested, provided 70% of the area was thriving. The state forestry department was charged with supervising the compliance of this act. In 1931 and 1934, inspections were made, certifying that the company efforts were satisfactory. The Ryderwood plan was to have planted 18 to 24,000 acres by the time the depression occurred. The primary method of reforestation during the early depression was by leaving seed trees along ridgelines for natural seeding. This practice continued throughout the early depression period.

With the newly planted forests, fire protection was of prime importance. Long-Bell, had become a member of the Washington Forest Fire Protection Association. Under association rules, each company was responsible for their logging operations; but the association protected the green timber. Logging railroad right of way, were converted into firebreaks and roads after logging had been completed. The ability to move quickly when a fire was reported was extremely important. Logging crews became fire crews in the event of fire. In addition the company maintained fire lookouts at Abernathy Mtn., Boist Fort Peak and two other locations. Air patrols were inaugurated in 1925 throughout the Pacific Northwest. These planes did not fly regular patrols; but were used in extreme fire danger.

With the return to better times and World War II, the company went back to emphasis on forestry and increased planting of its cutover lands. By 1950 clear results of the early efforts in planting were showing up. Consideration was given to thinning operations in selected stands. A stand of 60 year old Douglas Fir was selected, about 60 acres. The stand was first entered in 1945, and several thousand feet of saw logs were removed. In 1949, thinning was continued with 3,495 poles and piling taken out for the Longview treating plant. The trees were selected to aid the growth of those left and let in sunlight to the entire tract. The 1949 cutting yielded 366,970 feet of logs.

In 1951, 82,501 acres of company timber lands were certified as tree farms. Ryderwood had 65,702 acres, Grand Ronde (Polk County, Oregon) 18,899 acres and increased to 27,000 acres in 1975. It was fitting that the tree farm designation came at the 75th anniversary of Long-Bell. By 1961, the company had 7 designated tree farms, Ryderwood, Grand Ronde, Lower Umpqua (Gardiner), Smith River (Gardiner and Vaughan), Vernonia and Weed (Klamath Unit, Scott Valley and Weed). By 1973, the Ryderwood area was almost completely reforested with 28,000 acres being hand planted along with some aerial seeding. The balance was essentially seeded from blowing seed from ridge top seed trees. (11)

The efforts toward planting in the South produced similar results, with the first nursery at Longville, Louisiana in 1927. The nursery provided the first seedlings in 1929/1930, with 2.6 million seedlings planted on 2,800 acres averaging 912 seedlings per acre. Cost of planting was $11.13 per acre including seedlings. Southern soil was not always suitable for planting; but in this experiment, the program was considered a success. Studies made in 1942 show the average height at 22 feet but some as high as 42 feet in Slash Pine stands. Some of the plantation was located along Highway 170, serving to educate the public as it grew. The first thinning occurred in the 1940's, cutting posts, poles and pulpwood. Major cutting occurred in 1956 when posts and poles were harvested. Between 1956 and 1973, 30,000 poles, 3.7 million feet of timber, and 18,000 cords of pulpwood were harvested. This tract, as well as those across the south was managed on a 25/30 year cycle. Although Long-Bell was a follower in the south on reforestation, the role they played in the west, proving that planting young seedlings on cut over land was a long term benefit, would eventually move the entire industry toward forest renewal.

Acknowledgements;

1   Log of Long-Bell, June 1925, Page 20/21

2   Log of Long-Bell , November, 1923, Page 2 to 4

3   Log of Long-Bell, January, 1926 , Page 20

4   Log of Long-Bell, September, 1925, Page 16

5   Foresters Report on Longview Timberlands, Internal Document, June 23, 1925

6   Foresters Report on Longview Timberlands, Internal Document, June 23, 1925

7   Log of Long-Bell Log, August, 1925, Page 2/3

8   Log of Long-Bell, March, 1926, Page 6/7

9   Log of Long-Bell, February , 1928, Page 18/19

10   Longview Daily News, November 2, 1933, Page 1

11   Long-Bell Log , January , 1951, Page 1 and 5

Tree Planting at Ryderwood 1925
Courtesy of the Longview Public Library

Chapter 14

TROUBLE AHEAD
REDEMPTION AT LAST

When Long-Bell decided to make the move to the Northwest, they envisioned the opportunity to continue profitable operations, created by the southern mills. With World War I over, pent up demand for domestic and potential for strong export markets beckoned. Rebuilding war torn Europe would need large volumes of lumber for construction. New markets in Japan, China and Australia would create opportunities for timbers and other items, with South America, South Africa, and other locations all needing additional supplies of lumber. With the new mill at Longview being situated on the Columbia River, Long-Bell was poised to be a major shipper into export, East Coast and California markets.

In 1924, the year Long-Bell started production at Longview, Washington the West Coast Lumber Association reported 7,876 million board feet were shipped to the following markets.

2,057 mm f.b.m.	California	(1,621 mm f.b.m by water)	
1,264 mm f.b.m.	East Coast	(1,027 mm f.b.m by water)	
613 mm f.b.m.	Japan	365 mm f.b.m.	Egypt
203 mm f.b.m.	Australia	189 mm f.b.m.	West Indies
167 mm f.b.m.	China	169 mm f.b.m.	Central America
69 mm f.b.m.	Hawaii	53 mm f.b.m.	Europe
19 mm f.b.m.	So. America	10 mm f.b.m.	Cuba
9 mm f.b.m.	So. Africa	7 mm f.b.m.	Panama Canal
7 mm f.b.m.	Philipines	4 mm f.b.m.	New Zealand
3 mm f.b.m.	South Seas		

(f.b.m is feet board measure. m equals thousand feet, mm equals million feet)

In addition, 36 mm board feet were shipped south of the Mason Dixon line, with the balance by rail throughout the United States. Long-Bell, with its vast sales force, quality and service intended to be in all markets in order to keep the mills operating at capacity. (1)

Slow lumber markets prevailed from 1919 through 1922, but by 1923 and continuing through 1929, the nation's lumber mills produced over 30 billion feet a year, based on U.S. department of Agriculture sources. With the nation's economy booming markets for lumber flourished. The year by year volumes are listed as follows. (2)

1923	37.2 Billion	1927	34.5 Billion
1924	35.9 Billion	1928	34.1 Billion
1925	38.3 Billion	1929	36.9 Billion
1926	36.9 Billion		

With declining production from Southern mills, the time seemed right for Western mills to produce generous profits. However this was not to be, as obvious signs of over production were abundant. Operators continued to reduce asking price levels, until many were selling below their cost. Very few who had cheap timber could record a profit, as meager as it was. Mill operating schedules were reduced or curtailed. Long-Bell had hardly started up their mills to full capacity, before curtailments began. It was common practice to operate six day weeks at eight hours a day. Saturday work would be curtailed; but often an entire shift might be shut down for a week at a time. This was hardly an auspicious beginning, for a new, high cost modern mill. The West Coast lumber situation was courting disaster, despite the seemingly buoyant market. In 1926 27 % of the West Coast mills were closed, 30.1% in 1927 and 28.8% in 1928, grim evidence of a very unhealthy condition. (3)

By early 1926, there were attempts by major producers to merge their companies. By controlling this amount of production, management could alter volume to the flow of the market. In theory it looks good; but seldom worked out the way it is planned. The companies involved were major producers on the West Coast and included Portland Manufacturing, M&M Woodworking, Nicolai Door, (all Portland,Oregon) Wheeler Osgood (Tacoma,) and Henry Mc.Cleary Timber (Shelton and Mc.Cleary, Wa.). The proposal had a capitalization of $10, million; but for a variety of reasons the merger did not move forward. (4)

During this era, it was common for logging camps and mills to see downtime in the winter. Some of the larger companies had the ability to shift logging to lower elevations; but they also lost time. Long-Bell announced they would no longer work on Saturday, due to market conditions.

Long-Bell and other producers were constantly looking for ways to cut cost.

By late 1926, the need to combine production was more acute than ever. W. B. Greeley, Secretary/Treasurer of the West Coast Lumbermen's Association was strongly agitating for a combination of producers and often spoke out for outright government control of the Douglas Fir industry. In the fall of 1926 70 mills, planned to merge which would involve approximately a third of western production. Key members were in discussion with the major banks, with the intent being to stabilize the lumber market. The 70 mills consist of 41 companies including most of the major companies of Oregon and Washington; but did not include Long-Bell or Weyerhaeuser. Among them, C.D.Johnson, Toledo,Oregon, Bloedel Donavon, Seattle, Washington, Oregon American, Vernonia, Oregon, Charles Nelson, San Francisco, California, W. A. Woodard, Cottage Grove, Oregon, Westport Lumber, Portland, Oregon, St. Paul @Tacoma Lumber Company, Tacoma, Washington, State Lumber Company, Vancouver, Washington, Blodgett Company Grand Rapids, Michigan, Willapa Harbor Lumber Company, Raymond, Washington, Pacific Spruce Lumber Company, Portland, Oregon, Tidewater Lumber, Portland, Oregon , Cobbs and Mitchell, Portland, Oregon, Silver Falls Lumber, Silverton, Oregon, Umpqua Logging; C. H. Wheeler Lumber, Portland, Oregon ,Fir Tree Lumber, Booth Kelly Lumber, Springfield, Oregon, Crossett Western lumber, Weston Lumber, Owen Oregon, Medford, Oregon. The merger never came to fruition. One of the major points of contention was who would be running the new enterprise. (5) There had been many rumors concerning Long-Bell being involved in merger talks with someone, due to meetings in California, with all the senior managers being involved, the rumors were strongly denied. (6)

Western lumber companies were always at the mercy of the national railroad system on freight rates and the supply of boxcars. Constant negotiation, for lower freight rates to Midwest, Southwest and Eastern markets seldom met with success. Compounding Long-Bell and other major producers problems of excess production, was the proposed mill complex by Weyerhaeuser Timber Company on land optioned from Long-Bell in Longview, plus new mills at Klamath Falls, Oregon and Lewiston, Idaho. The Weyerhaeuser directors continued to hedge on when the complex would be built, causing Long-Bell consternation, as they had hoped to sell housing lots to Weyerhaeuser employees.

The year 1926 saw a total of 689 sawmills cutting lumber in the state of Washington as compiled by Abbey Lumber Register. In addition, there were 532 planer mills and wood working plants, 185 shingle mills, 65 box plants, 20 veneer mills, 16 pulp and paper mills, 19 door plants 13 sash and frame plants 8 garage door plants, 19 cross arm plants, 4 handle mills, 13 cooperage plants, 10 wood preserving plants, 57 furniture factories and 586 logging camps. Supporting these facilities, were 58 company stores, 98 hotels and boarding houses, 124 camp mess halls, 261 wholesale lumber companies and 201 machine shops.(7)

Early 1927 saw more curtailments in order to stabilize the market. Throughout Washington, mills were down for a week or longer. Long-Bell curtailed four days to allow inventory balance. By early 1928, the company shut down the night shift due to weather and M. B. (Mike) Nelson Long-Bell president called for industry reductions. By August, 1928 the East sawmill night shift was cancelled and the balance of the complex was running at 70% capacity.(8) Mills that belonged to the W. C.L.A. had capacity to produce approximately 250 million board feet a week from 226 mills. The weekly production levels averaged 60 to 70% of capacity depending on the time of year. By October 1929, it was only 50% of the 1926/1929, weekly average capacity.

The West Coast lumber industry tried a variety of schemes to increase price levels and production, most were ineffective In 1929, The Douglas Fir Exploitation Company was formed, to serve as a clearing house for export business under the Webb-Pomerane Act. Long-Bell and Weyerhaeuser were both members. (9) Other attempts at regional selling combinations, under the same act were tried with little success. The W.C.L.A. assessed its members .05 cents per thousand board feet, to develop an advertising program, to combat substitutes. This assessment would generate $700,000.and allow the association to add 25 field men and generate advertising. Since 1909, lumber consumption had declined by 20% and substitutes had increased by 29 %. A major factor in the increase of substitutes was the use of metal in automobiles which had replaced wood. Running boards, spokes for wheels and part of the auto dash board all had been predominately made of wood construction.

Economic conditions throughout the country were not robust in the late 1920's. Continued short closures of mills occurred throughout the spring of 1927. In mid summer of 1927, a giant rail merger was announced, with Great Northern, Northern Pacific and Chicago Burlington and Quincy prepared to join together. Again competition and costs were pushing these companies to merge. The combined capitalization was about $5 billion. The merger did not come to pass at that time; but the thought continued as they did eventually merge in the late 50's or early 1960's.Business news continued to be discouraging as the Milwaukee Railroad system fought to avoid bankruptcy.

Despite the rather frequent accusations of collusion among lumber producers, as it relates to price levels, the lumber trade remained chaotic. Reduced demand for housing, a slowdown in oil well drilling in the southwest and lack of demand in foreign markets all took a toll on production. It seemed that the mills were always looking for a disaster to bail them out. That philosophy remains today. Starting with the massive San Francisco earthquake, then the

Yokohama earthquake of 1923, mills would rush to satisfy the need, only to fall back when price levels collapsed due to over production.

The late 1920's had a profound effect on the profitability of west coast sawmills. Most mills were selling below cost, operating part time. Long-Bell mills ran at about 75% capacity. With the company's extensive retail system and Weyerhaeuser having a solid network of field salesmen, they probably fared better than most; but not much. Long-Bell would not post a profit on the Longview operation until the early 1940's. (10)

The stock market crash in October, 1929, reverberated throughout the lumber industry. Collapse was at hand. The further into the depression, the faster mills closed or drastically curtailed. At the end of January, 1930, production was running at 75/80% of the 1926/29 weekly average. Out of 778 mills, 68 were closed. It would worsen rapidly and by the end of 1931 mills were operating at 42% of capacity with only 222 mills reporting to the W/ C. L. A. The operating statistics were somewhat misleading, as many mills did not report their production to the W. C. L. A. Mills cutting as little as 5 to 20 thousand board feet a day and Tie mills cutting for Japan, China and domestic markets were not included. The weekly statistics listed down and operating together, so the situation was much worse than it appeared.

The collapse of the lumber market was not limited to the West Coast species, as Southern Pine, Western Pine and Hardwoods were suffering also. Lumber inventories at mill locations were climbing rapidly and it would be a serious factor until the lumber code authority took effect. Data developed during W. H. Cronwall's investigation of Long-Bell finances show the following:

Industry Lumber Inventories in Equivalent Days Production as of April 22, 1932 indicate the dire situation of the industry.

	Southern Pine	West Coast	Western Pine	Hardwoods
6-29-29	62 days	46 days		147 days
6-28-30	88 days	62 days	177 days	184 days
7-4-31	85 days	61 days	177 days	218 days
4-2-32	87 days	60 days	151 days	233 days

The situation would not improve until actual The Lumber Code Authority quota allocations were imposed in 1933. The quotas factored in individual mill inventory situations when allocating production volume and hours. (11)

Reviewing production statistics from the years 1926, 1930 and 1937/1938 as reported by The Timberman magazine indicates the rapid reduction in volume and number of mills that occurred during this time. Total volume produced by the top 20 mills in the Douglas Fir region was 1926, 3.247 billion feet, 1930, 2.340 billion feet, and in1937 and 1938, 1.311 billion feet. Every company involved in producing Douglas Fir would be affected. (12)

By the end of 1931, mills were running at 25% of capacity, with price levels of West Coast lumber averaging $20.48 in 1930, down to $13.96 at the end of 1931. At this point, most mills were down or severely curtailed. Both Long-Bell and Weyerhaeuser were curtailed by mid 1930. Long-Bell had shut down the West mill night shift, joining the East mill curtailment. (12) W. B. Greeley Secretary/ Treasurer of the West Coast Lumbermen Association, was still pushing for consolidation in the industry and government intervention. At the beginning of 1932, the industry had 675 mills with 291 not operating, The W. C. L. A estimated that mills were losing 2 to3 dollars per thousand and the industry has lost $6 million dollars on 3 billion feet of timber produced. Prices are about $5.00 below the 1930 levels. Many companies are operating just to keep employees and communities afloat. Jobs were being shared, working 3 days one week and 2 days the next. Wage levels were steadily reduced, often down to 20 cents per hour.

Small spurts of business offer some encouragement; but too quickly the gloom returns. Export volume dries up as British Columbia mills have a $4.61 dollar freight advantage over West coast mills and with the worldwide depression, the British Commonwealth drew together and what little business that was available, was sent to British Columbia mills. In January 1932, production was at 22% of capacity, by mid July, 1932, it was at 15.7% of capacity. (13)

In 1932 some relief begins to show, with a new lumber tariff on Canadian lumber which drastically slows volume by month from 70 million feet a month to 7 million feet. Protracted negotiations have resulted, in substantial rate reductions from the railroads into the Eastern sector of the country. Lumber production at the end of 1932 was 19.3% of capacity. With a new administration elected, the lumber industry felt that the bottom of the depression had been reached. Production had reached a final low of 17.8% of capacity from 172 mills producing 39,527,000 feet. (14)

With a new administration in 1933, the lumber industry finally had hope that something could be done to rectify their overproduction and employment problems. Thousands were out of work and wage levels were less than 50% of the 1926/29 period. The new administration set out to return the unemployed back to work, raise and stabilize wages and give the populace purchasing power. The National Recovery Act was passed establishing a code of conduct and operation of each industry. A lumber code of practice, was established which controlled production, established minimum wage levels and opened the door for labor to organize and bargain collectively. (15)

The code was controversial but needed to allow mills to return to profitability. The code would have complete control of wage levels, hours of production, volume produced and the minimum selling price. The most difficult factor in developing the code was the wide range in wages paid between the West Coast and Southern mills. Southern Pine and West Coast lumber was highly competitive. Southern Pine had a distinct freight advantage; but higher timber costs. West Coast lumber had higher labor and production costs but lower timber costs. Southern mills often worked 60 hour weeks versus West Coast at a 48 hour week. Oregon and Washington with 26,300 fewer workers produced 2.6 billion feet more lumber than Southern mills for the same time period. Wages in the South averaged, $ 9.18per thousand feet or 33.8% of total cost, while West Coast was $10.93 or 52.4% of cost.(16)

With the implementation of the lumber code, the number of producing mills rose rapidly. The code virtually guaranteed mills a profit. Production reported to the W. C. L. A in late January 1933, went from 172 mills upward to 356 by September, to 476 mills by early January 1934. Weekly production volume over the same time period went from 39,527,000feet, to 92,351,000 feet in late December 1933. 1934 was the high point of the lumber code era, as 570 mills were operating with production rates of 80/100,000,000 feet a week. The code listed every operating mill, compared to previous volumes only reported W. C. L. A.

Despite the cessation of the lumber code in 1935 and controls that went with it, conditions began to improve. With early 1933 being the low point of the depression, slowly the situation improved. By mid 1935, mills began to add curtailed shifts and weekly production began to rise. Year to date, weekly average production as reported by the W. C. L. A. was 68,361,782 feet at 202 mills. By year end, 1935 production had risen to 103,000,000 feet weekly average. With the exception of a short summer slump, when Long-Bell shut down for a week, 1936 proved to be a stable year. Production was increased by 26% over 1935. A lengthy Longshoremen strike, seriously affected the results; but Weyerhaeuser reported that profits were on the increase and Long-Bell began to show improvement in their financial problems. (17)

By mid- summer 1937, lumber markets began once again to decline. Long-Bell and Weyerhaeuser were operating 32 hours a week and were seriously considering wage reductions, as the nation began to see signs of a reoccurrence of the depression. By the end of 1937, mills were operating at 39 % of 1926/29, average weekly production. W. C. L. A. mills reporting on a weekly basis fell from 202 to 149. (18) Labor unrest continues to build as mills offer wage reductions or closure. The business slump continued through spring and early summer 1938. However by midsummer, the market firmed and mills that had been closed for over a year began to reopen.1939 saw stable production early in the year; but with the start of World War II, in Europe, volume and price levels began to climb. Weekly production levels of 133,818,000 is 68 % of the 1926/29 average and water shipment increased. The federal government begins to increase purchases for defense needs of lumber products.

With the federal government actively involved in lumber procurement, operators are flush with business. With this success, came government control, price ceilings and serious disruptions to domestic needs. With the entry into the war, the war labor board takes full control over all lumber production, bringing back a bureaucratic approach to all transactions, which was similar to the control under The Lumber Code. Early in 1942, mills were operating at 245/247,000,000 feet weekly average; but by late fall, with mill workers and loggers being drafted into the services and serious production declines occur.

During 1943 through 1945, production levels fluctuated widely, due to lack of manpower. The mills hired women to augment the labor shortage and the working age was lowered to 16 years of age. Part time shifts were offered to alleviate the bottlenecks in the mills; but the shortage of loggers was felt everywhere.

Government purchases of lumber had thrown regular production schedules out of kilter, due to extremely high demand for 1" boards, needed for crating and packaging. With the tight supply base, the government built its own mill (Youngs Bay Lumber Company) in the Roseburg, Oregon area, with production being primarily boards. Labor strife was rampant in the Northwest over wages. The war production board refuses to allow wage increases and freezes workers to their jobs. Lumber production had been tightly controlled, by the war production board; but occasionally lumber grades not needed for defense use were released to the retail trade. This would normally cover grades number3 and number 4.With timber supplies dwindling, mills on the lower Columbia began to close, Clark and Wilson who operated mills at Prescott and Linnton, Oregon, closed as did Westport Lumber Company. Clark and Wilson lost enough timber in the Tillamook area fires to last 20 years at both mills. (19)

With the end of World War II in sight and dropping of controls by the war labor board, the lumber industry was ready for a long period of prosperity. Certainly the war years saw price levels high enough to make profits; but with adequate labor available and the nation converting to peacetime activities, the path forward was to be rewarding.

Sources:

(1) Longview Daily News, April 25, 1924, Page 6

(2) Cronwall Report, Exhibit 50 C

(3) Timber and Men Hidy Hill and Nevens, Page 434

(4) Longview Daily News , January 19, 1926, Page 1

(5) Longview Daily News , September 24, 1926, Page 1

(6) Longview Daily News, February 12, 1931, Page 1

(7) Longview Daily News, June 6, 1927, Page 1

(8) Longview Daily News, August 3, 1929, Page 1

(9) Longview Daily News, May 22, 1929, Page 1

(10) Cronwall Report, Page 75

(11) Cronwall Report, Exhibit 50 GG

(12) Timberman Magazine January 927, Page 50, January 1931, Page 163 and January 1938 Page 24@28

(13) Longview Daily News, July 16,1932, Page 6

(14) Longview Daily News, February 12, 1932, Page 6

(15) New Deal Lawyers Peter H. Irons, Page 17/18

(16) Longview Daily News, August 28, 1933,

(17) Longview Daily News, August 31, 1935, Page 7

(18) Longview Daily News, December 18, 1937, Page   7

(19) Longview Daily News, December 29, 1944, Page 1

Chapter 15

LUMBER CODE AUTHORITY

With the crushing depression beginning in 1929, the commercial world seemed to come to a stop. Massive unemployment, slashed wages for the ones still employed and nationwide labor unrest called for drastic measures by the new administration in the spring of 1933. The Roosevelt administration set a target of 100 days to develop and enact legislation designed to stabilize wages, increase employment and eliminate the suffering of the past 3 years. Since the 1929 crash, 13 million workers lost their jobs and industrial wages fell from $17 billion to $6.8 billion. (1)

President elect Roosevelt's advisors advocated a massive public works program. Finding jobs for the unemployed was of prime importance. The Civilian Conservation Corps was the first program enacted, employing men 18- 26. The initial stages would employ 250,000 and eventually grow to 500,000 men and operate until World War II started. The second major program to be initiated was the National Recovery Act (N I R A). The new administration was looking for ways to jumpstart the economy. A model for halting the industrial decline was a program used during World War I, the War Industry Board, which was used by the government to coordinate production and procurement of essential war time goods. The administrative structure of the War Industry Board rested on collaboration between federal officials and industrial trade associations to which power over industrial production was delegated by presidential proclamation. President Roosevelt was well informed about the War Industry Board workings, having served as assistant Secretary of the Navy during WW I, and also as head of one of the industry trade associations. He fully intended to use this program as a model for the recovery. (2)

The industrial leaders who supported the New Deal proposed a plan of political- economic corporatism based on relaxation of anti-trust laws and   a system of business and government collaboration of production and prices. The industrialists were to accept government regulation and agreed that the real solution was to forget about competition and concentrate on government controls. Eliminating cutthroat competition, which forced under cost, price cutting was the major goal. The term adopted was industrial self- government. Industry operating codes were to be developed. Major efforts to suspend anti- trust and price fixing enforcement would be inserted into the individual codes. (3) During the 1920's, the federal justice department was zealous in prosecuting anti- competitive schemes.

With the new administration under pressure to develop solutions to ease the pain of the depression, President Roosevelt pulled his chief legislation writers together, which was three separate groups and told them to lock themselves in a room and not come out until they had agreement on a suitable piece of legislation. The key intent of the code authority bill was to create a method to re-employ laid off workers and enable the work force to return to better living conditions.

The key bill, which related to production control, fair pricing and wage and hour standards, was presented as " Codes of Fair Competition" and had been proposed by trade associations and other industry groups. Definitions of what constituted fair competition was left to the individual code drafters. Equally important, was that the proposed bill suspended the enforcement of the anti- trust laws against industries covered by a code. Undefined monopolies were prohibited and codes were required not to oppress small enterprises. (4)

Two other provisions of the legislation authored by General Hugh Johnson, satisfied the demands of organized labor, that it include language that labor would have a guarantee that workers could organize into unions and bargain collectively with employers. This portion of the bill became section 7(a) of The National Act. The second important point was the inclusion in the bill, of a section for a substantial publics works program, which we know as the WPA. (5)

The drafters, of this National Recovery Act, left broad discretionary powers, to the president on developing the administrative structure. The drafters of the bill also armed the president with wide powers to force reluctant industries into line. One provision authorized the president to impose a code on an industry, if its representatives could not reach agreement on one and another provision empowered the president to enforce compliance through a federal licensing agreement.

Little thought was put into the bill as it related to constitutional questions. Several questions were raised; but with the pressure to make something happen, these were left un- answered. Suggestions were made that congress set wage and hour standards, industrial prices fixed at 1929 levels and production restricted to 55% of the 1929 level. None of these suggestions lasted through the legislative process. The N.I.R.A. act passed the House of Representatives in late spring, 1933, 323 to 76, and passed the Senate June 16, 1933. (6)

Every industry was to have a code, which resulted in hundreds, then thousands of codes to develop and administer. This meant developing administering codes throughout all industry down to the community level including stores and business. With the N.I.R.A. bill adopted, General

Hugh Johnson, selected to head the agency, declared that the top ten industries would develop their codes first and become the model for the others to follow. Cotton and Textile were the first developed with Coal, Petroleum, Iron and Steel, Automobiles and Lumber to follow. (7)

The adoption of the N.I.R.A. legislation proved to be a nightmare to administer and a bonanza for employment of lawyers and legal personnel needed to develop the codes, prosecute violators and administer this new agency. A major problem in the code development and enforcement was that the justice department offered little or no help or support when disputes arose. Despite the passage of the N.I.R.A., the act did not replace the anti- trust laws in effect. The Justice Department was charged with upholding these laws, so in effect the justice department was either on the sidelines in cases involving litigation or in some instances actual opponents at times. The entire legal staff associated with the N.I.R.A. had little or no experiences in litigation that would go to the Supreme Court. Another obstacle to smooth progress was that Federal Judges who would rule in most cases on the litigation were predominately appointed by previous administrations who were not sympathetic to the N.I.R.A. act and often ruled against the cases brought before them.(8)

The development of the N.I.R.A. code of practice would substantially change business practices. Definitive government control would dictate how much an individual mill could produce, hours of operations, minimum wages and initiate labor bargaining units across the entire country. It would not be business as usual.

The nation's lumber business could not be in any worse shape. For years, the key lumber associations had been advocating consolidation and reduced production. Several major attempts at industry restructuring in the late 1920's, resulted in only exploration and talk. W. B. Greeley, Secretary/Treasurer, West Coast Lumbermen Association, frequently advocated for government control without any resolution. Construction of housing (the major use of lumber) fell to 15% of normal in the early 1930's. Lumber production fell drastically, to a low of 18% of the 1926/ 1929 weekly average.

Developing a code for the lumber industry would cover 36,000 companies and over 400,000 employees. The code would affect every company who logged or produced products made of wood across the nation. Basic industries such as sawmills, plywood, veneer, flooring, doors, windows, wooden boxes, pulp and paper, garage doors, cooperage, treated, cross arms and a myriad other end use would be covered by the code. Due to the many competitive factors between geographic regions of the country, each major producing area was set up as a region with local specifics being incorporated into the code. (9)

Fourteen specific producing regions or industries have been identified, with all of them subject to the code. The key elements in the identified areas are, the minimum wages paid by area and the maximum hours worked weekly. Each region developed its own code, addressing the peculiarities of the region or product.

Wage and Hour Section

1) Northern Hemlock 48 hour week, 22 cents per hour minimum lumber manufacturing, logging 22.5 cents per hour

2) Northern Pine 48 hour week, 32.5 cents per hour lumber, 25 cents logging

3) Northwest Softwoods 40 hour week 22.5 cents per hour logging, 25 cents lumber

4) Redwood 48 hour week lumber, 40 hour logging, 32.5 cents per hour

5) Southern Pine 48 hour week, 22.5 cents per hour

6) West Coast Logging and Lumber 40 hours lumber, 48 hours logging, 40 cents per hour factory workers, 42.5 cents lumber and logging

7) Western Pine 48 hours logging, 40 hours lumber, 42.5 cents per hour except New Mexico and Arizona 48 hour week, 22.5 cents per hour

8) Western Red Cedar Shingles, same as west coast logging and lumber, except 40 cents per hour for stained shingle division

9) Woodworking Industry 40 hour week average for 6 month; but a 48 hour maximum. Sawmill same as woodworking except 25 cent absolute minimum with no more than 25% of total work force at minimum class.

10) Veneer Industry 44 hours in southern zone at 25 cent per hour minimum, 40 hours in northern zone at 30 cents per hour and 40 cents per hour in metropolitan cities.

11) Oak Flooring 48 hour week, In towns less than 5,000, 22.5 cent per hour, 25 cents per hour from 5,000 t0 50,000, 27.5 cents above 50,000

12) Walnut 40 hour week, 25 cents to 40 cents same as veneer

13) Hardwood 48 hour week, 22.5 cents per hour with 25cents in north central and northeastern mills

14) Mahogany 40 hour week, 30 cents per hour in southern zone, 40 cents in northern zone and 45 cents in Philippine Mahogany industry

Putting all these factors into a workable code would prove to be impossible. Wage levels were set at a 1926/1929 average. (10)

Based on the peculiarities within each region, the code developers had three factors to consider, maximum hours worked each week, minimum wages and acceptance of labors right to bargain collectively. The regions met in mid- summer 1933 in Chicago, Illinois to come up with an overall code acceptable to the government, not an easy task. The coordination of this task was done under the umbrella of the National Association of Lumber Manufacturers.

Heading up the entire effort was J. D. Tennant, Vice President and General Manager, Western Operations of Long-Bell. He was also former President of the West Coast Lumbermen Association for the previous three years. He was an excellent choice as he had spent many years in the Southern Pine industry and had credibility with the southern producers. Other Long-Bell officials involved with the process of code development were, C. E. Lombardi of Long-Bell's legal staff and Weyerhaeuser involved, J. P. Weyerhaeuser, Laird Bell and A. W. Clapp (11)

The code consisted of 10 articles which included minimum wage and maximum hours worked, production control, minimum price levels, forest conservation, trade practices, standard grades, standard forms, accounting, re-inspection and claims and rights of labor to organize unions and negotiate working agreements.

The administration of the code would be supervised by the major trade associations, IE: West Coast Lumbermen, Western Pine and Southern Pine associations etc. Nationally, the code organization was managed by David T. Mason, a renowned forestry consultant (Mason /Girard), Portland, Oregon. (12)

Obviously the establishment of the code would allow price fixing, in the guise of minimum prices, giving the producing mill an opportunity to finally return to a profitable basis, as the mill costs were known. A key factor in the minimum was to assist paying the highest possible wages, in order to give the wage earner money to spend.

The lumber code covered the major industries of lumber and logging, however there were many specialized operations that came under the major industry umbrella. The Northwest Door and Softwood Plywood industries were left out of the original discussions, yet they needed to be included. In order to simplify the process, the two associations merged to ease compliance under the code.

One of the issues addressed in developing the code, was forest conservation. For many years concerns about running out of timber, over cutting, tax issues and re-forestation were discussed in lumber circles, congress and concerned individuals. Gifford Pinchot, former head of the Forest Service and former President Teddy Roosevelt were long time critics of logging and misuse of the nation's forests. Critics in congress were concerned with the destruction of forestland. Long-Bell determined in the mid 1920's that the company must involve itself in reforestation. Weyerhaeuser had also taken steps to extend the life of their company through reforestation. (13)

As part of the lumber code proceedings, a 16 point program, article 10 was proposed as part of the code, and included sustained yield, conservation of young trees, cooperative fire and other forest protection, taxation reform and disposition of cut over lands which had been returned to tax rolls. The final draft of the code included these points and the procedures to enforce it. (14)

By the end of June, 1933, 1000 lumbermen gathered in Chicago, Illinois to resolve the differences between the 14 regional sections and come up with a single code acceptable to all. The code was to be supervised by a board consisting of 24 members. An emergency committee was formed to coordinate between the lumber producers and other industries covered by the code. The federal administration strongly preferred a single code covering all industries under the wood products entity. Key industry leader's, felt that the code, gave the opportunity for self regulation; but also imposed the duty of self restraint. (15)

J. D. Tennant, chairman, proposed using wage levels for the year 1926, as this was the most prosperous period of the decade. By mid July, the code was submitted to the N. I. R. A. administration, being the second group to file a code. The wage scale was almost double 1933, as the administration was pushing for more purchasing power by individuals. Included in all codes was a provision that child labor was prohibited under the age of sixteen.

Minimum prices were to be set, which provided the producer a return over costs, returning most mills to a profit after many years of operating at a loss. The committee felt that the code as presented was the best they could do.

With the code submitted to the administration, the lumber industry urged its acceptance and implementation. Workers being well aware of wage levels suggested were anxious to begin collecting the benefits. Mill operators were also ready to reap the higher prices, not seen for a long time. Wilson Compton, President of The National Lumbermen's association, stated that lumber producers did not share in the boom of 1923- 1929 and was unprepared for the depression that followed. He also pointed out, the perilous condition in the lumber and timber industry, with ten billion dollars, invested in timber ownership, mills and distribution of the product. These mills provide employment to hundreds of thousands employees in regions which had little, if any other industrial development.

As of July 21, 1933, the National Recovery Act Lumber Code went into effect, with problems still to be resolved. Considering the distances traveled and communication difficulties of the era, this was a major accomplishment. The Lumber Code had its share of detractors and opponents. Labor opposed the wage scales, as not being in the spirit of the recovery, maintaining proposed wages did not lift the workers above subsistence levels. Western producers protested the low wage levels of the Southern producers, claiming it was unfair competition. Southern producers rebutted that Southern cost of living was much lower, which was not acceptable to the new administration. The code was not embraced by several large Western producers, who claimed they would need to lay off workers in order to comply with code provisions. Even though problems existed and disagreements were numerous, implementation proceeded. With the enactment of the National Code structure, the new administration hoped to see six million employed.

Despite the urging of J. D. Tennant, Chairman of the Lumber Code Authority and his executive committee for quick approval, General Johnson rejected the code over the wage differential between West and Southern operators. Workers across the country were well aware of impending increases in hourly wages to comply with the proposed codes. Operators were concerned about labor disruptions across the entire industry and walkouts did occur at Klamath Falls, Oregon and Grays Harbor, Washington mills, which increased the pressure. Many operators including Long-Bell and Weyerhaeuser increased the wage level to 42.5 cent an hour in anticipation of code acceptance, while others increased to 32.5 cents an hour, with back pay to come if code approved.(16)

On August 19, 1933, the lumber code was approved and sent to President Roosevelt for signature. Final adjustments were made on wages and hours with West Coast at 42.5 cents an hour and a 40 hour week except in seasonal periods when climatic conditions make longer hours necessary and the wage rate in the Southern Pine region rose to 23.5 cents per hour. Production control was to be managed by the administrators of the code, in the case of West Coast lumber, the West Coast Lumbermen association. Regardless of whether a mill belonged to the association or not, its production allocation was distributed, through this method. August 22, 1933 the code became effective, with 115,000 men employed. West coast workers (40,000) would have more money to spend. Mill operators awaited instructions on how the various code provisions would work. Thirty eight distinct wood products industries are covered by agreement, the most important were Lumber, Logging, Shingles, Plywood, Sash and Doors and pulp and paper. (17)

While the Lumber section of the code was drawing the most attention, other segments of the industry were developing their own particular codes. The code for Pulp and Paper was ready for acceptance. Locally, Longview Fiber, Pacific Paperboard and Weyerhaeuser Pulp were involved. Wage levels were to be 35 cents for males and 30 cents for female workers in all mills across the country, except for two areas in the south where males would be 32.5 cents and females 27.5 cents per hour. In the Longview area, Weyerhaeuser Pulp would add another shift and hire 40 workers, while Longview Fiber would work six hour shifts and add 100 men, in order to comply with the code. (18)

With the implementation of the code, administrative activities swung into action. Allocation for September production was set at 450 million feet, with 120 hours of production allowed. Mills would work a 30 hour week, six hours a shift. This would be the first time in many years that West Coast mills, had been able to control production and not build inventory. The labor committee of the

National Code Authority ruled that Planer mill workers would be paid 42.5 cents an hour, rather than the 40 cents being paid factory workers, no distinction to be made between male and female workers on wages. Office employees of lumber and logging companies to receive no less than 42.5 cents an hour and 40 cents in factory positions, with maximum of 40 hour work week. It was noted that all code violations will be given immediate attention by the secretary and if necessary by the entire code committee. By mid September, 1933, the west coast region was busy settling minimum price levels for all markets, determining fair operating practices, final grading rules and other issues pertinent to putting the rules into action. (19)

In Longview, Washington, at a local community discussion J.D. Tennant, Chairman of The Lumber Code Authority told how the code was formulated. He indicated that there were 30,000 sawmills in the country, with 20,000 of them having an investment of less than $5,000 dollars. The industry employed over one million men and in some cases wages jumped 200/400%, as some wages were as low as 5 cents an hour, working 60/72 hours a week. (20)

One of the articles incorporated into the National Lumber Code was section 7A, giving labor the right to organize and negotiate collectively. This section would cause considerable consternation among the producers. West Coast mills who were involved with unions, were satisfied with the 4-L Union (Loyal Legion of Loggers and Lumbermen) which was company controlled, having management on the steering committee. With implementation of the lumber code, organized labor was quick to begin organization efforts throughout the West Coast.

The implementation of the Lumber Code was not without protest. The first protest came from the President of Coos Bay Lumber Company, W. B. Denham, Coos Bay, Oregon who was a vocal objector when the code was being formulated. Willamette Valley Lumber, Dallas, Oregon filed suit against the West Coast Lumbermen and N. I. R. A. over 120 hour operating limit. The new schedule called for one shift, a week operation, while previously the mill worked two shifts 48 hours a week, employing 530 men. The code authority did not increase Willamette's production quota. (21) Westport Lumber, Westport, Oregon had the same complaint. Lumber wholesaler's who usually purchased direct from the mills and were left out of the code, now had to buy from retail yards, another problem to work out. The lumber industry did not like the code; but couldn't survive without it.

The lumber code staff assembled data on a quarterly basis, dealing with lumber production, shipments, inventory, booked orders on hand, possible future demand and other factors. Based on these findings, a national quota would be set for the next quarter and divided by the various components such as west coast, western pine, southern pine, redwood, etc. In turn, the quota was allocated to the individual companies by the regional agency (West Coast Lumbermen in case of Douglas fir) for the next period. The quotas probably erred on the side of optimism, in order to maximize employment and partially to avoid difficulties in compliance and enforcement. Conflict was inevitable, as the W. C. L. A. tended to favor the small producer in allocations. A compromise needed to be worked out, as the major employers employed the most workers. (22)

One of the most controversial sections of the lumber code was price control. Minimum prices were established for 97 components of the code and 87,000 individual items. The system worked for about a year; but by June, 1934, it began to disintegrate. Initially the wholesale operators were left out of the code, so they were not subject to price control however the code was amended where the wholesaler had to purchase his product from the retail yard, which did not work either. Total enforcement of price control was not effective and criticism by government officials undermined the effectiveness of the program. (23)

So strict was the code authority that individual mills were not able to expand without approval of the code authority. Absolute control over how much was produced was the goal. As the system took hold, slowly the volumes were increased. By the start of 1934, volume allocated was about 25% better than weekly volume of 1933. Violations continued to occur and in the West Coast region, kept under control. In the case of Willamette Valley Lumber, the presiding judge stated that the lumber code was not perfect and some may suffer more than others. He also pointed out, that in 1929, 95,000 were employed with a payroll of $120 million dollar's, while at the end of 1933, only 10,100 were still working. The 30 hour work week was established because it was the only equitable working scale for employees and operators. (24)

Production quotas continue to fluctuate with business conditions. While business had improved, it was too early to tell if the code had provided the emphasis for improvement. Labor unrest was causing disruptions, as section 7a, which is part of the recovery act, took the attention of the labor force. By mid- summer 1934, due to the slump in the lumber market 1934, mills were only working 24 hours a week, rather than the 30 hour week prescribed in the code.

Despite the obvious facts that the code rescued many mills from oblivion, dissension among producers, wholesalers and others continued to grow. J. D. Tennant, Chairman of the code authority was a strong supporter even though it did not allow Long-Bell to operate at the level needed to survive. Others felt major changes were needed. A summer review session revealed that many were ready to quit the process, due to numerous claims of cheating on prices and production volume. Code management did not want the pricing problems to show up in court as a test had never been made to determine if price fixing was legal. Retail dealers and wholesalers were the biggest culprit, pushing consumers to buy hand to mouth expecting a major price adjustment. Prices were adjusted downward and the wholesale segment added to the code where they belonged.

A major disruption in the enforcement of the code was the existing legal system. With the establishment of the National Recovery Act, a multitude of lawyers and legal assistants were hired to develop and administer the codes. Realizing that disputes would occur, an attempt to work closely with the Justice Department was made. There were many features of the code structure that the Justice Department disagreed with, especially the price fixing aspect. The N. R. A. in most cases chose to take their cases to court, rather than ask for help from the Justice Department. Professional jealousy, often stepped between the two groups, resulting in defeat after defeat for the N. R. A. staff. Few were experienced in courtroom litigation. (25)

As 1934 drew to a close, dissension grew rapidly against the code. Violations were numerous and cheating on price was rampant. Petitions were being circulated throughout the West Coast to do away with the fixed pricing system. In mid September, 1934, seven Lumber firms were charged with selling below fixed price minimums. Five of the firms were from Tacoma, Washington and had been selling below the levels for several months. This action was a major factor in demoralizing the other producers. Operators in the Portland, Oregon district, petition the lumber code authority to revoke the minimum pricing section of the code. The petition indicated that the enforcement of the code would require a major increase in staff to audit the price levels. (26)

Southern lumbermen joined the protest, filing suit asking for an injunction to prevent any enforcement or prosecution of violators. C. C. Crow, of Crows Lumber Journal polled the western industry on the minimum pricing issue and claimed 83% were against price fixing. Throughout the fall of 1934, continued calls for abandonment of price fixing were made. Weekly, additional companies were cited for violations, 20 in the Portland, Oregon District, 3 in Seattle/ Everett, Washington and 5 in the hardwood district. By late October, 1934 the industry was in full revolt. At a meeting held in Tacoma, Washington, W. C. L. A. trustees voted 14 to 7 to eliminate price fixing. The staunchest supporters including J. D. Tennant and W. B. Greeley could not convince the dissidents to hold the line. By mid December, 1934, The Lumber Code Authority asks for enforcement or abandonment of the price fixing section. Many Southern mills were working 50/60 hours a week and paying as low as 10 cents an hour. (27)

The year 1935 opened with the price fixing clause still alive. David T. Mason, Lumber Code Administrator, said code enforcement is definite and if regional agencies can't handle the enforcement, the government will. With this announcement, the national code authority took over administration of the code of Georgia- Florida Hardwoods division. (28)

Unsettled lumber prices had serious side effects as mills began to curtail rather than continue to produce at a loss. Long-Bell was discussing wage reductions in March of 1935, with revisions to the code promised. Steps were taken to meet justice Department objections. A case before the Supreme Court against Belcher Lumber Company of Alabama for violating the wages and hours provisions of the lumber code were dropped by the N. I. R. A. effectively destroying any ability to enforce any section of the code. (29) By early April, 1935 a vote was taken within all agencies of the lumber code on whether to continue or abandon the code, 56 voted to abandon, 36 to continue, 14 non- committal and 33 not responding. Government response was the code will continue; but would not enforce the minimum price fixing issue. By the end of May, 1935, the codes for all industries were abandoned, due to lack of suitable enforcement by the federal government. Strong resentment was felt by the lumber code staff and its supporters, feeling that the federal government, through the N. R. A. administration, had sabotaged the efforts of the lumber committee. The government response was that the lumber code was a voluntary effort and should have been under government control all along. With the abandonment of the code system, the National Recovery Act effectively died. (30)

Despite the turmoil and infighting caused by the formation of the code, lumbermen around the nation took up the challenge to develop a workable system. Western Pine, Northern Hardwood, Northern Hemlock and Redwood, all felt the code worked well for their organizations. The national lumber situation demanded some type of control, as the sheer number of lumber operations precludes any freedom of normal competition. There will always be someone lower in price, different cost structure, raw material prices, etc. to make competition on a national basis impossible. (31)

West coast operators had about one year and a half of stable pricing at levels high enough over their costs to allow a return to profit for many operators. By 1935, there had been enough upward price movement in market conditions, to allow operators to see improvement, despite the limited production levels imposed by the lumber code administration. The improvement in markets would continue into late 1937, and despite the many labor disruptions, allowed many to return to profitability. The lumber code, considering the immense number of products, the task to administer was impossible. Considering the magnitude of the task at hand, it is no wonder that it unraveled after just a little over a year.

Addendum

When the Lumber Code Authority was formed under the auspices of the National Recovery Act, the lumber industry became hostage to strict regulation. Every aspect of the operation was spelled out how an individual company could operate, through hours worked, log volume allowed and production volume for each mill. In the case of the West Coast mills, the W. C. L. A., was the allocating source. Throughout the nation, the leading trade association was chosen to administer the code whether the individual mill was a member or not. The administrators took the allocation given to their association and divided it between the mills registered as participants. Often the national code office was over optimistic in their allocation, resulting in fewer hours worked than planned. Examples of specific allocations indicate the level of detail involved.

Longview Daily News 2-17-1934

The Lumber Code Authority has allocated the following for mills in the mid Columbia area of Washington and Oregon. Mills will work 30 hour weekly schedules. The mills listed include every mill that qualified, whether large or small. The designation m, equates to thousand and mm, equates to million.

Aagard-Charleston (K) 1,960 mm, R. M. Adams #1 (K) 780 m , E. H. Adams #2,(K) 878 m, R. O. Bicknell (W) 390m, Castle Rock LBR. (C) 195M, Closner Bros. #1(Ke) 288m, Closner Bros. #2 (Ke) 356m, W. E. Craik #1 (W) 780M, W. E. Craik #2 (W) 780M, O, W. Curtis (Ke) 390m, Davis Broth. (C) 127M, Lee East 7 mills, (C) Feb. and Mar. 1,296 mm, J. B. Frost (W) 351M, Kelso Lbr., (Ke) 522m, E. R. Kramer (Ke) 293m, Lewis and Karn (L) 390M, Lindsey, Shatter (C) 585m, Long-Bell East Fir (L) 19,868mm, Long-Bell West Fir (L) 25,123mm, Charles Lyon 4 mills (Ke) 2,340 mm, A. C. Majors (O) 390 m, A. M. Mead (Ke) 293m, Morgan @ Son (Ke) 390 m, Ostrander Timber (O) 2,693 M, h. A. Pellet (Ke) 510 m, Rowell-Markle (K) 1,526 m, Snyder@Dougherty (O) 488 m, Weyerhaeuser (L) 57,245 mm, George Youst (W) 225 m.

The above serves as an example, as to what transpired each month or quarter, for logs, lumber volume, hours or shingle volume. The parenthesis reflect where the local mill is located . K stands for Kalama, W for Woodland, C for Castle Rock, Ke for Kelso, L for Longview and O for Ostrander, all located in Cowlitz County. The designation (m) stands for thousand board feet, (mm) stands for million board feet. During this period of time, Cowlitz County had mills located as follows:

Kalama, 5 mills

Woodland, 4 mills

La Center 1 mill

Kelso, 8 mills

Ostrander 3 mills

Longview 5 mills

Castle Rock 9 mills.

In the smaller communities, most of the small mills were cutting Railroad Ties.

References

(1) The New Deal Lawyers Peter H. Irons Page 17

(2) The New Deal Lawyers Peter H. Irons Page   17/18

(3) The New Deal Lawyers Peter H. Irons Page   19

(4) The New Deal Lawyers Peter H. Irons Page   22

(5) The New Deal Lawyers Peter H. Irons Page 22

(6) The New Deal Lawyers Peter H. Irons Page 23

(7) The New Deal Lawyers Peter H. Irons Page   31

(8) The New Deal Lawyers Peter H. Irons Page 31

(9) Forests For The Future Rodney C. Loehr Page 101

(10) The Timberman Magazine   July 1933 Page 8

(11)Forests For The Future Rodney C. Loehr Page   100

(12) The Timberman Magazine   July 1933   Page 6/10

(13) The New Deal Lawyers Peter H. Irons   October 24, 1933 Page 1@7

(14) The New Deal Lawyers Peter H. Irons   June 30, 1933 Page   1@11

(15)   The New Deal Lawyers Peter H. Irons July 1,1933 Page   1

(16) The New Deal Lawyers Peter H. Irons   July 31, 1933 Page 1

(17) The New Deal Lawyers Peter H. Irons   August 19, 1933 Page   1

(18) The New Deal Lawyers Peter H. Irons September 1, 1933 Page   1

(19) The New Deal Lawyers Peter H. Irons August 30,1933   Page 1

(20) The New Deal Lawyers Peter H. Irons September 7, 1933 Page   5

(21) The Timberman Magazine   November 1933   Page 76

     The Timberman Magazine   February 1934   Page 63

(22) Forests of The Future Rodney C. Leohr Page 101/102

(23) Forests of The Future Rodney C. Leohr Page 103

(24) Longview Daily News January 24, 1934 Page 3

(25) The New Deal Lawyers Peter H. Irons   Page 11/13

(26) The Timberman Magazine November 1934   Page 81

(27) The Timberman Magazine   October 1934   Page   52/53

(28) Forests For The Future Rodney C. Loehr   Page 150

(29)   Forests For The Future Rodney C. Loehr   Page 152/154

(30)   Forests For The Future Rodney C. Loehr   Page 158

Also:

The Battle For Democracy Rexford Tugman Page 5, 17-20,43

Chapter 16

FINANCIAL DIFFICULTIES

In the late 1800's, with the rich supply of natural resources and the rapid movement of people into the mid and southwest sections of the country, it was an opportune time to start a new venture. R. A. Long and his associates developed a highly successful company from the very beginning, generating profits which were quite satisfying up to the terrible depression of the 1930's. As the company grew, expansion through building new sawmills, adding retail yards or expanding into new product lines such as Treated, Hardwood and the Weed acquisition were generally financed through issuance of corporate bonds. In the early days of the company, new mills were often acquired, purchasing a controlling interest in the venture. Bonds sold in 1909, for a value of $ 9 million dollars had been paid down to $ 226,000 in January 1921. The company always paid their debts within the schedule agreed to.

The company was well managed and financed. There was nothing on the horizon to indicate the trouble that lay ahead. Southern mills and the Weed operation continued to generate profits every year up through 1929, whereas the Longview operation was a significant drain on corporate profits. From the very beginning, the Longview operation was in financial trouble. Over production of West Coast lumber was evident in the early 1920's. Mills were selling product below cost in many cases, just to generate cash flow.

The expense of building the new mills at Longview, building the city and its infrastructure and the need to put levees around the entire valley, cost Long-Bell far more than they had originally planned. The company issued new bonds in the early 1920's for $ 10 million dollars. Based on an article in "The Long-Bell Log", the bonds sold well in face of a weak market for this type bond. (1) The bonds were sold in denominations of $1,000, $ 500 and $100 dollar increments. This certainly did not indicate the troubles that lay ahead.

By the late 1920's, the situation began to change. The southern lumber operations were limited to Lufkin and Doucette, Texas and Quitman, Mississippi, with Hardwood operations at De Ridder, Louisiana, Helena, Arkansas and Doucette, Texas. In addition, Weed, California, the Retail Yard chain,

Treated, Sash and Door and Company Stores remained profit contributors against the drain on earnings by the Longview operations.

The situation at Longview grew worse, as curtailments occurred on a regular basis. Normal operating schedule in the 1920's was six days at eight hours per day. With the constant fluctuation in the lumber market, curtailing sawmill operations was used to balance the flow of product through the rest of the mill. The company had planned to operate the mills at full capacity, which would be approximately 550 to600 million board feet a year, on a two shift basis. The results were not close, as the mill produced 319 million board feet in 1926, 386 million 1927, 417 million 1928, 334 million 1929, 252 million 1930 and 201 million feet in 1931.

With serious deterioration of the lumber market, Long-Bell was concerned with making payments on their timber contracts with Weyerhaeuser. Early in 1928, Long-Bell had asked Weyerhaeuser Timber Company for relief on a portion of their existing contract for Ryderwood timber and the relief was granted. In September, 1928, Long-Bell once again came to Weyerhaeuser, stating they would like to skip payment of the October timber purchase amount of $ 765,112. but would pay the interest. This was a clear indication of how severe the situation had become.

Price levels deteriorated during this time, with prices for the total product average moving from $22.13 per thousand board feet in 1926, $ 20.91 in 1927, $ 20.65 in 1928, a high of $22.97 in 1929, $19.13 in 1930$ 14.31 in 1931 and $ 12.35 in first half of 1932. (2) From 1930 forward the losses would be severe, considering log costs, labor, overhead and other charges. By August 1928, Long-Bell reduced the work schedule to five days and in 1929, curtailed the night shift of the East Sawmill, shifting the crew to other jobs on the mill site.

By 1930, the company reports a loss in the third quarter of $688,869. and it would only get worse. The company negotiated the sale of the mill site powerhouse to Washington Gas and Electric in November 1930, the price received was less than what it cost to build. (3) In October 1930 on advice of bankers, The Long-Bell Sales Corporation was formed which took over all the company assets except for the timber.(4) The idea was, this would allow the company access to banking lines of credit not presently available to Long-Bell Corporation. This arrangement would last until the company was reorganized.

The company tried everything possible to reduce costs and generate a profit. Hourly wages and salaries were cut as the depression worsened. In 1931, The Longview Portland and Northern Railroad was sold to The Northern Pacific, Great Northern, Union Pacific and Milwaukee railroads and the company used the proceeds to pay off a gold note of $3.5 million dollars.(5) The 1930 loss was reported at -$ 3,736,000, 1931 at -$ 7,992,000, 1932 at -$5,018,552 and 1933 at -$3,685,207.

An editorial in the Longview Daily News, 12-21-31, pointed out, that Lumber sales return was $ 13.43 per thousand feet, versus an average cost of $15.55. Another serious problem for the industry was inventory of unsold lumber. At year end 1931, Southern Pine mills had 164 days of production in inventory, Douglas Fir 143 days, Western Pine 401 days and Hardwoods 452 days at the present rate of consumption. (6) Mills were operating to allow their employees with a way to survive. Job sharing was utilized to employ the greatest number possible. Long-Bell was working five day, 6 hours per day schedules.

By late 1931, Long-Bell was desperate for cash, running at a deep loss, just to generate enough to stay current. They turned once again to the bond market, putting up the company for collateral to sell $ 20 million in bonds. By early 1932, they missed interest payments and two of the 8000 to10,000 bond holders sued to force the company into liquidation. A bondholders committee was formed in an attempt to keep the company intact, with a plan, toward re-organizing the company. The lawsuit filed by the two dissident bond holders was settled in Long-Bell's favor, with a clear path clear toward gaining new financing and the re-organization of the company. The company was valued at $ 85 million dollars with outstanding bonds of $ 20 million and indebtedness of $ 22 million dollars. The company had not paid a dividend since 1927, with wages and salaries reduced and strict control of spending practiced.

In January 1932, the company announced they would not be able to pay $ 173,625.interest due February 1, 1932; but did pay the January interest.(7) The bondholders who filed suit against the company went back to the courts and petitioned for the company to be placed into receivership. M. B. Nelson, president said it was not necessary as all debts would be paid. On April 1, 1932 an amended petition was filed by the original bondholders claiming that the company had transferred assets of Long-Bell Lumber Company to the Sales Company leaving only the timber as assets of the lumber company.(8) The majority of the bondholders favored re-organization and by May, 1932 had accumulated 70% of the outstanding bonds $ 14,091.million and working to collect the balance. The bonds were needed to keep the company in daily operating funds.

In October 1932, in a series of hearings on receivership of the company, M. B. Nelson testified to salary cuts made since 1930. Reductions were made, 10% in July 1930, 10% November, 1930, 10% April 1932 and 25% in June 1932 and everyone including R. A. Long were affected. The salary reductions of 52.16% coupled with wage reductions of 45% for hourly workers were to save over $1 million dollars. (9) R. T. Dempsey, Vice President, testified that company sales in 1926 were $ 22, 344,000 but had declined by 1931 to $8,559,000 and down to $ 2,596,000 in the first six months of 1932.

October 15, 1932, a federal judge denied the dissident bondholders suit for receivership of Long-Bell, opening the way for re-organization. By spring, 1933, the Bondholders committee and Long-

Bell executives began discussions on re-organization. Views on company bankruptcy had changed drastically across the nation as a result of the disastrous depression. It was much better to save a company than destroy it.

The Bondholders employed a management consulting firm, S. C. Cronwall, to investigate Long-Bell from top to bottom in order to determine if the company could be salvaged or sent into liquidation. Every aspect of the company, timberland, sales, manufacturing and management were reviewed and a schedule of recommendations provided to the committee for their decision. The review was most thorough in its scope, with detailed reviews of every operation, including closed or abandoned facilities and timberlands with recommendations for disposal or continued operation. Backup data, including lumber statistics on production volume back to 1900, with each of the major producing regions listed was provided. Most of the recommendations were accepted and implemented in the final accord. (10)

Long-Bell stockholders not only suffered from the company woes but also through rapid deterioration of the stock value. All of the officers held shares in the company, as did many regular employees. The company had been selling stock to them for many years. The stock price reached a level of $32.00 in 1928 to 1929; but would be seriously affected by the 1929 market crash. Price declined to 4 ¼ in 1932 and 7/8 during 1935, remaining at very low levels until 1940 when it began to improve.

The year 1933 has been considered the worst year of the depression, with sawmills operating at 18/25% of 1926 to1929 levels. With the landslide election victory of the Democratic Party and Franklin D. Roosevelt as a crusading president, there was hope for improvement. A series of work generating programs was quickly enacted, with the Civilian Conservation Corp Act as the first piece of legislation, followed quickly by The National Recovery Act and the Lumber Code. The goal was to increase wages and employ more workers; but also guarantee producers a profit. For the first time in a long period, mills could sell for more than it cost to produce. Although brief in its structure, the Lumber Code was a distinct benefit to Long-Bell.

By late 1933, a letter to the bondholders outlined the progress being made by Long-Bell and the Long-Bell Sales Company. A voluntary re-organization would best conserve the assets of the company, especially the first mortgage. The committee had appointed Halsey-Stuart Company, Chicago, Illinois as re-organization managers. A preliminary outline of the re-organization had been negotiated with creditor banks and others. It provided for dissolution of the Long-Bell Sales Company, cancellation or modifications of contracts and obligations and creation of new securities to replace the existing first mortgage bonds and bank debt. Through excellent cooperation with Weyerhaeuser Timber Company, a contract for 58,415.27 acres of timber was cancelled with a value of $11,584,124.01.(11) This tract of timber had been purchased in 1928 as the second of two timber purchases from Weyerhaeuser. A contract for timber with the Milwaukee Land Company, for $500,000., was agreed to, returning uncut timber back to Milwaukee. With these agreements, the company would still have access to 5.8 billion feet of timber.

The company and bondholders through Halsey-Stuart were actively pursuing the recommendations of S. C. Cronwall management consultants. In April M. B. Nelson, President of the company, pointed out in the annual report that much progress had been made in straightening out the affairs of the company. (12) Losses continued with cancellation of timber contracts and charge off for land scheduled for abandonment, raising the deficit for 1934 to more than $ 9 million dollars. The balance sheet indicated $ 22 million in long term debt and nearly $11 million dollars in current liabilities. Capital stock was at $ 52 million and a deficit of $ 18 million. Total assets were $62 million compared to $ 100 million in 1932 and $ 116 million in 1930. (13)

In August 1934, Long-Bell slashes real estate prices in Longview, by up to 70%, with the sale to last 60 days, with an additional 20% off for cash. The intent was to reduce housing inventory and taxes. (13) As a sign of better things happening, the company paid $ 40,391, the current and delinquent taxes to Lewis County, Washington. In March 1935, the company was set to implement the re-organization, establishing a board of control, consisting of three bondholders and two from Long-Bell to be approved by Federal Judge Merrill Otis. The chairman of the bondholders was James M. Kemper, President, Commerce Trust Bank, Kansas City, Missouri, the other members were J. Z. Miller, former member Federal Reserve, E.C. Cronwall, Chicago,Illinois, experienced in timber finance and brokerage and for Long-Bell, J. L. Westlake St. Louis, Missouri active in the building of Longview and Jessie Andrews, General Counsel.(14)

In March 1935, the final re-organization plan was presented to Judge Otis. Approval would mean bondholders would receive preferred stock to the value of bonds held and par value equivalent in common stock as default interest. Current bank debt, slightly less than $4.5 million was converted-Into installment unsecured notes payable from 2 to 10 years. The company emerged as a 46 million dollar company, free of debt and possessed of working capital for major operations. (15)

During the two years of study and restructuring, the market had begun to improve. The Lumber Code Authority certainly assisted Long-Bell's financial situation, until the code was abandoned. The market was showing new life, with mills long dormant starting back to work, increased retail yard purchasing and higher price levels. As a sign of improvement, Long-Bell contracted for the entire output of the J. H. England mill at Winlock, Washington for a period of several months. Volume was about 80 thousand feet a day and would be shipped in the rough to Longview for finishing. (16) Long-Bell also paid $ 89,800 to Cowlitz County for back taxes, making them current. Lewis and Wahkiakum counties also received $75,000 each for taxes owed. (17) In late December 1935 all aspects of the re-organization were approved. Long-Bell was discharged from all previous debts and liabilities.

With the exception of a slump in business in late 1937 through the summer of 1938, the lumber business was finally operating in good shape. Lumber markets grew at a good pace and with war clouds looming in Europe, export shipments increased dramatically. As the United States began to rearm, defense orders began to take preference, with the Longview operation running close to capacity. Company reports indicate quarterly profits, enough to begin retiring preferred stock. Six months into 1941, 7,810 shares had been retired and by year end 3,490 more. (18)

By November 1941, the profit picture had changed enough, that the company paid out a $ 5.00 preferred dividend. All outstanding notes had been paid. Net earnings after taxes, for first nine months of 1941 were $ 2,423,518., compared with $337,230 in 1940. By year end the company had $ 2.6 million to buy up preferred stock from a sale of Arkansas and Louisiana second growth timberland. (19) In December 1942, Long-Bell acquired Polk Operating Company, Polk County, Oregon which was indicative of their improved financial condition. In January 1943, Weyerhaeuser Timber Company purchased the Reservation tract of timber from Long-Bell. Located north of Klamath Falls, Oregon, it was considered to be too distant for use by the Weed, California operation. By February 1933, another dividend, $ 12.14 on preferred stock, was paid.

Indicative of the greatly improved condition of Long-Bell, was a report that Longview shipped 518 million feet in 1943, of which 60 million was purchased from other sources.(20) In March 1943 the night shift of the East Mill resumed operation having been down since the early 1930's. The addition will add 35/40% to the plant capacity and in April 90 men were added to the West Mill night shift.

On March 28, 1944, court control of Long-Bell ended. Having satisfied all their court imposed obligations, Judge Merrill Otis dissolved the board of control, which was set up as part of the re-organization. The bondholders turned over to Commerce Trust Company, $237,626. and 30,216 shares of stock. (21) On March 30, 1944 the company declared their first dividend, 10 cents a share on class A and 10 cents on common stock, the first since 1927.

Despite price controls and defense purchasing during the war years, Long-Bell returned to strong financial performance. Primarily with funds generated from cash flow, acquisition of Vaughan, Austa, Gardiner and Vernonia properties were made from 1946 to 1953. Record breaking sales and profits were being made year after year. Unfortunately Mr. Long was not able to enjoy it having died in 1934, in the depth of the company troubles.

Sources:

1 Log of Long-Bell   August 1922   Page 9

2 Cronwall Report Long-Bell Shipments by principal product and prices received   Exhibit #34

3 Longview Daily News November 1 1930   Page 1@5

4   Longview Daily News October 25, 1930 Page 1

5   Longview Daily News September 23, 1930 Page 1

6 Cronwall Report   Exhibit # 50GG

7 Longview Daily News   January 28, 1932 Page 3

8 Longview Daily News May 28, 1932 Page   1

9   Longview Daily News   October 6, 1932 Page 1

10 S.C.Cronwall Report   unnumbered pages

11 S.C.Cronwall Report   Pages 98/101

12 Longview Daily News April 11, 1934 Page1

13   Longview Daily News August 4, 1934 Page 1@2

14   Longview Daily News March 9, 1935 Page 1

15 Longview Daily News March 23, 1935   Page 1@5

16 Longview Daily News   November 29, 1935 Page 1@9

17 Longview Daily News December 23, 1935   Page 9

18 Longview Daily News July 26, 1941 Page 6

19 Longview Daily News November 5, 1941 Page 8

20 Forests For The Future, David T. Mason   Page 224

21 Longview Daily News March 28, 1944 Page 1

Chapter 17

LABOR RELATIONS

The manufacturing of lumber throughout the South occurred primarily in isolated areas with the company building the mill responsible for the development of housing and community infrastructure in most cases. The end result was that employees would be at the mercy of their employer. The employee rented from the company, purchased his groceries at the company store and worked the hours the company demanded (usually 11 hours a day, six days a week). Long-Bell entered into lumber production with the knowledge of how the system worked.

Communities developed by Long-Bell seemed to have more resources than the average company town. As a result, the labor force was better off than other communities. Long-Bell paid the employees in cash rather than script or tokens, as tokens were always a point of contention at other mills. The wage level during the early 1900's was $1.50 to $1.70 per day for common labor. Skilled labor would receive $3.00 to $5.00 per day, with saw filers commanding $7.00 a day. Labor turnover rate during this period was 14% to 16%, with White workers moving more than Black or Mexican labor. In most sawmills, 60% of the jobs were considered common labor, with lumber graders, saw filers, sawyers and mechanics being considered skilled.

Attempts at union organizing had been made prior to 1900, with local coal mines being organized; but the lumber companies had too tight a grip on the sawmill communities to allow organizers any leeway. With conditions exceedingly poor across the timber belt, agitation for union organization reached its peak during the 1910 to 1914 period. The Brotherhood of Timber Workers was formed, targeting the mills of East Texas and Louisiana, seeking better wages, working conditions, relief from predatory pricing practices at company stores and a shorter work day and week at same pay. (1) Long-Bell management was very concerned about the threatened union activity. C. B. Sweet, Vice President of operations was a key member of The Southern Lumber Operators Association, consisting of all the major producers throughout the South. This group was well organized and stood together to combat violence and attempts to organize the labor force. Black lists were organized and a clearing house was established at Alexandria, Louisiana to prevent union sympathizers and organizers from moving between mills. (2) In June 1912, violence erupted at Grabow, Louisiana a few miles outside De Ridder, Louisiana resulting in several deaths. The operators decided that the troubles had gone far enough and a steady process of curtailment occurred throughout the South. Mills began operating four days a week instead of six to discourage the labor agitation.

The Long-Bell mills were in the center of labor agitation, despite the improved living conditions. The Industrial Workers of The World (IWW) had become part of the organizing attempt and were well known for their harsh stand and radical position. The Southern Operators Association shut down eleven mills in the most troubled area around De Ridder, with The Hudson River mill being affected. (3) There were 300 mills ready to close down and the mills that were closed stayed down for seven months. The mills were filled lumber and the market was in the doldrums, so mill operators could bide their time. This action finally broke the attempt to unionize the south. A small benefit came from the effort with a slight increase in pay and a ten hour day.

There were further attempts to unionize the South; but market conditions favored the mill operator's ability to curtail production and thwart any serious efforts toward unionizing. In the period 1919 to 1920, the American Federation of Labor made an attempt to organize skilled workers; but again the operators closed ranks to freeze them out. Long-Bell Board of Director notes in 1917 indicate the tightening of labor supply, which lead to increasing wages to $2.00 per 10 hour day and a 10% increase for salaried workers. (4) R. A. Long pressed mill managers to upgrade living conditions in company owned housing, seeking to keep labor peace.

With the assumption of financial control over the Weed Lumber Company, Long-Bell took on a new set of labor problems. Although prior to 1917 the area around Weed was relatively trouble free from labor dispute, it was about to change. Partially due to World War I and the unfavorable attitude toward foreign workers and the rise of the Industrial Workers of The World, troubles began. Weed management reported that attempts to start a fire in the planning mill had been thwarted and Pinkerton detectives were hired to investigate the incident. This occurred in April, 1917. Through active agitation by the I. W.W., the mill was forced to increase wages to $3.25 per day. Reports of wages as high as $ 4.00 a day at Oregon mills circulated frequently. McCloud Lumber Company, twenty miles to the East of Weed, imported 300 black laborers at $2.75 per day to offset the increased cost. (5)

As Weed Lumber Company became more sophisticated and departmentalized, labor problems surfaced. The operation at this time consisted of a Sawmill, Green Chain, Stacking Yards, Lath Mill, Plywood Plant, Door Plant, Box Plant and a Window Sash Plant. Moving employees between these different units was often difficult; but usually without problems. In 1919 Weed employees organized a union, International Union of Timber Workers #114, with virtually all of the hourly workers electing to join. On March 6, 1922 the union called a strike over reduction of wages and extended working hours. The strike lasted six weeks, with the mill operating the entire time, hiring new employees to replace the strikers. Long-Bell imported Black workers from Louisiana and Texas, advancing moving costs, to be paid from wages earned. Eventually the strike ended, with over 100 workers leaving the area and the balance returned to work. The outcome of the strike was that mill management felt that the main instigators of the strike were from the Italian community and a black list developed. The list carried 147 names as undesirable and not to be hired back, with nine names to be investigated prior to being rehired. The list is still in existence as part of the Weed Historical Society display at Weed, California. The former employees on the black list were forced to move out of company housing or from houses the employee built on company land. As a result of losing the strike, the union dissolved. (6)

In 1937/1938, Lumber and Sawmill workers local 2907 of the American Federation of Labor began signing up workers. On October 20, 1941 another strike was called by the 1100 workers over seniority, a wage raise to $.70 cents per hour, union shop and one week paid vacation. The strike lasted until December 15, 1941 when both sides agreed to federal mediation. The union was awarded all their demands except union shop. However a union security shop was granted, requiring all workers who had belonged to the union at the beginning of the strike to pay dues; but new hires were not required to join the union. The strike was a success due to racial harmony in contrast to the 1922 strike.

When Long-Bell moved to the West Coast, they were looking for labor peace. In the extensive investigation of the move west, labor supply and union activity were considered in the decisions on where to locate the mills. The West Coast had been beset by labor troubles, as conditions were harsh in the logging camps and mills. During the period, 1910 to 1918, the I.W.W. labor union was active, organizing the mills and camps. Strongly influenced by Communist leanings, the union was the scourge of the operators. Their influence was so strong, that in many communities, the local Sheriff waited at the train station and hobo camps to warn suspected union organizers not to get off the train. The situation became so serious during World War I the Federal Government stepped in as I.W.W labor disruptions in the Spruce Logging camps was delaying production of Airplane Spruce.

Under the direction of Bryce Disque, Colonel in the U.S. Army, the military took over the logging camps on a temporary basis. A union was formed to combat the effects of the I.W.W. and was called the Loyal Legion of Loggers and Lumbermen, or 4-L union. It was truly a company style union, as it had representation from both labor and management on the steering committee.

The 4-L union was what Long-Bell faced as they started up the mill operations in

Longview. Being a company union, labor was not satisfied with their lot. Leading up to the depression, there was plenty of labor strife. The Shingle Weavers union was very active, with strikes occurring throughout Western Washington and Northern Oregon, dealing with wage increases and union or closed shop operations. The operators resisted fiercely. Locally the Kalama,Washington area was the most active with Barr Shingle Mill opting for an open shop: but paying higher wages as an incentive. Disgruntled Barr employees created acts of vandalism, including dynamite. Despite the strong lumber and shingle markets, by 1929 signs of trouble were occurring as mills cut production and initial wage reductions began.

Beginning in early 1927, Long-Bell and others curtailed production, adjusting to a slow lumber market. By the spring of 1929, West Coast mills were running at 70% of capacity. In July 1930, the 4-L union launched a protest over wage reductions, from $3.40 per day down to $2.50/3.00 per day. At a meeting in Longview, Washington, 750 mill workers and families protested living costs in the area. (7) Workers received $60 to70.00 a month in wages but living costs were $80/100.00 a month. Long-Bell being the major landlord, reduced rents by 10%, making it the third reduction for a total reduction of 45%. Washington Gas and Electric also made reductions. By 1931, the State of Washington had 85,000 unemployed, having doubled the unemployment rate of 1930.

With the crash of the 1929 stock market, lumber activity declined rapidly. In the spring of 1930, a woods hook tender was paid $9.60 per day; but by the end of the year, the pay was lowered to $4.60 per day. Lower skilled loggers were paid 22 cents an hour and the individual logger was forced to work seven days a week just to pay his room and board at $1.35 per day. (8) The 4-L union had tried to hold out for a $2.60 per day minimum; but soon operators cut the pay to $1.50 a day, causing the union to abandon the minimum scale effort. Looking for utopia, in 1929 the National Lumber Workers Union was formed. Their demands were for a $6.00 per day, double time for overtime, a work week of five days, with a total of 35 hour week, a seven hour day in the woods including travel time, abolition of the black list and elimination of the 4-L union. Needless to say, the union never got off the ground as an organization. One of the major factors, which thwarted union activity, was the large cadre of unemployed non-union workers. The operators used every tactic they could to discourage union activity, opting for the relative peace of the 4-L organization.

Labor was squeezed between the operators and the depression. Protests by the unemployed only caused the situation to worsen. Unemployed protests in Seattle, reputed to be communist inspired, brought out the police. Shingle Weavers in Grays Harbor struck over wage reductions, with continual clashes between strikers and those who want to work. Throughout all this labor unrest, the 4-L union remains ineffective. With the election of 1932, a new administration is installed with the avowed goal of reversing the effects of the depression. Legislation is enacted toward back to work proposals. A key piece of legislation, The National Recovery Act would generate a major beneficial effect for labor. In the act, Section 7A, provided labor with an unrestricted right to organize as a union and the right to bargain collectively with employers over wages, hours and job performance.

Nationally strikes over wage reductions and hours were widespread. Auto, steel, construction laborers, coal mine and rubber workers left their jobs in dispute over lack of jobs and low wages. Unions of the early 1930's were primarily craft oriented, with the mass production facilities not being organized or protected by union support. With the enactment of the N.R.A. (National Industrial Recovery Act) legislation, the American Federation of Labor was quick to react to the west coast lumber situation, enrolling thousands of lumber, plywood, loggers and shingle weavers into the union. Although the A.F. of L Carpenters and Joiners looked down on industrial workers, they did not refuse the dues potential. A major effort to organize sawmill and woods workers was begun in 1933, as soon as the N.R.A. was enacted.(9) Efforts in British Columbia to organize workers in 1931 to 1933 aided the move toward enrolling new members. One major factor in the A.F. of L reluctance toward recruiting industrial workers was the strong communistic influence, especially in the West Coast Lumber industry. Craft unions were strongly anti-communist and fought any perception of this influence. Union activity was slowed by enactment of the Uniform Lumber Code in 1933, which restored a minimum wage of 45 cents per hour, and set the hours of work per week. The code was established to equalize production with available business and return to employment as many workers as possible.

The first attempt at organizing Long-Bell and Weyerhaeuser hourly employees in the Longview, Washington area was in June 1933 with 400 employees attending a meeting sponsored by the A.F. of L Carpenter and Joiners Union. By June 27, 1933 plans to form the union were made. An organizational meeting was held at the local Y.M.C.A., with 800/1000 attending and the effort resulted in 332 signatures willing to join. (10) A charter granted by the A. F. of L would be the basis of the union, as most of those attending the meeting preferred the A. F. of L, to the existing 4-L union.

With the formation of the A. F. of L. Carpenters and Joiners union, the newly formed group came out swinging, advocating a 30 hour week in five days, 83.5 cents per hour or $25.00 a week minimum. The union was actively recruiting and had 1800 members as of July 1933, with the union local designated as 18260. (11) The union was also looking into hospitalization and state industrial insurance. Local 18260 vowed to cooperate with the existing 4-L union. Despite the efforts to organize the wood products labor force, the 1933 drive was not a total success.

Despite the drive toward aggressive union organization, the northwest lumber and logging industry continued to have unrest among the workers. Strikes plagued the industry with Southern

Oregon and Grays Harbor mills being disrupted. Other mills ran out of logs, due to local strikes. The labor disruptions were over the minimum wage levels, which were set under the provisions of the Lumber Code. The code had been presented to federal administration officials for acceptance; but the operators couldn't enact the new wage levels without final approval. The workers knowing what the wage scale would be were impatient for implementation. Approximately 3500 men were out on strike by the end of July 1933. (12)

Mill operators, including Long-Bell and Weyerhaeuser began to pay the new rate of 42.5 cents an hour minimum generally agreed to in the lumber code. This was with the proviso that if the wage levels were higher in the final code, they would pay the difference back to August 1, 1933. On August 19, 1933 the code was accepted and labor peace was achieved for the present. With the approval of the Lumber Code, employment picked up in the local area, as the mills recalled some of the laid off workers. New order flow improved as lumber dealers were forced to pay a minimum price set by the code. (13)

With the enactment of the N.R.A. act and section 7A, the right to unionize and bargain collectively, problems began to occur as various companies sought to ignore the provisions of the new law. Active discouragement by company officials toward union activity occurred at many locations. Some operators balked at the total lumber code authority and its restrictions on hours worked and labor provisions.

By February 1934, the local union activity had progressed to the point where delegates were chosen by A.F. of L. and 4-L locals to begin negotiations with Long-Bell. A total of 10 candidates were to be selected, 5 from A. F. of L and 5 from 4-L, with a total of 5 selected from this group. In the course of selection and subsequent voting, the 4-L union charged interference in the balloting. The final vote favored the A.F. of L.

1934 and 1935 proved to be very unsettling periods of labor unrest. In the spring of 1934, Longshoremen on the Pacific coast, struck over wages, hours and rotating crews. Also on strike, were the Fisher Autobody plant in Cleveland, Ohio and coal mines in Alabama and Roslyn, Washington. On March 15, 1934, Long-Bell workers chose the A. F. of L. as their bargaining agent. The local would be known as 2504. (14) By early May 1934, Longshoremen had all West Coast ports shut down. Locally some violence occurred as a result of the Longshoremen walkout but the end result was complete closure of all operations at Long-Bell and Weyerhaeuser including the pulp mill. Twenty five hundred workers was affected locally and 16,000 in the Northwest.

In June 1934, the Longshoremen strike turned extremely violent in San Francisco, California resulting in several deaths. Locally the A.F. of L. filed unfair labor complaints against Long-Bell and

Weyerhaeuser over violations of section 7A of the N.R.A. act, alleging discharge over union activity, discrimination and coercion of employees. Continued closure of the local mills affected the supply of fuel for homes and the mill powerhouse. Local mill workers maintained their support of the Longshoremen strike and by mid July 1934, 63 tidewater mills were closed. At the end of July 1934, the Longshoremen vote for arbitration of their grievances. After 84 days of being on strike work was resumed on the docks, with little change in the wages and conditions. The violence left several dead and many injured. The A.F. of L. was quick to seize the opportunity in organizing the woodworkers. The union had a recognizable presence as an established entity and much preferred over the I. W. W. or 4-L organizations due to the communist influence or being controlled by the company.

Labor troubles would haunt the West Coast operators into the 1940's as one problem piled onto another. A festering problem of conflicting influences between competing labor unions would be the most disruptive. With the A.F. of L. being a craft oriented organization, their focus was not on the mass production facilities, Coal, Steel, Rubber, Auto and other industries employed large numbers of workers who felt they were not being fairly represented by the existing union structure. During the 1920's and early 1930's the A. F. of L was the only organization labor could turn to for representation. Longshoremen and Teamsters had some autonomy but were a part of the labor umbrella. John L. Lewis of the United Mine Workers had been frustrated for a long time under the leadership of the A.F. of L. Feeling that industrial workers were being ignored, he began to agitate for an independent organization which began to appear in 1935/1936 as the C.I.O (Congress of Industrial Workers) and this schism in the ranks of workers would have a long range disruptive effect on Western Wood workers.

The A.F. of L under the guidance of A. W. Muir, director of union activity in the Northwest, was responsible for the rapid growth of the union. With the clout of section 7A of the N.I.R.A. act behind the union, he quickly moved to gain the recognition for the union and began the task of wage improvement. During late 1934 and early 1935, business conditions were stable; but began to sag by spring 1935. Mills were looking to reduce wages, not raise them. Labor unrest was rising, with strikes and other disruptions occurring throughout the Northwest. On February 14, 1935, in a rare display of cooperation, Long-Bell and Weyerhaeuser employees met at the Longview Y. M. C. A., to discuss ways of preventing further reductions. The session included representatives of The A.F of L, 4 L union and workers not represented by either union. A proposal to strike was presented and soundly defeated. In mid April, 1935, the A.F. of L. Northwest Council decided to present demands to the operators for a $.75 cents per hour minimum wage and a six hour work day, with a strike starting the first week in May if the offer was not accepted. The operators said they could not meet the demands. (15)

In late April 1935, frequent walkouts were occurring as various locals reacted to the lack of progress being made by the union and usage of non-union workers in some areas. By May 9, 1935 sawmills and logging camps were seriously affected by the scattered strikes. Knowing the lumber industry had improved from the depth of the depression, the workers were tired of subsistent wages. Labor expected the union to negotiate an agreement, which called for union recognition, a six hour work day, 5 days a week, time and one half for over time, seniority rights and a 75 cent per hour minimum wage. There was much dissatisfaction with A. W. Muir and the results that the union had accomplished. A. W. Muir wanted to avoid a strike if at all possible and presented an offer to the Longview local on May 10, 1935 which fell far short of the workers expectations. The offer was for a 5 cent an hour raise to 47.5 cents an hour, time and one half for over time, union recognition; but not a closed shop. (16)

The workers were so disgusted they rejected the offer without a vote and Long-Bell and Weyerhaeuser workers went out on strike. Both mill groups met to formally vote down the offer by a 9-1 ratio. On May 13, 1935 all operations for both companies were shut down, as labor walked off the job felt they had a strong case for rejecting the offer, citing that lumber prices had risen 42%, while wages had risen only 7%.(17)

In a matter of days, 90,000 woodworkers were on strike. Pickets blocked the entrances to mills across the entire Northwest. Localities which relied on power from mill sources scrambled to find alternative sources and homeowners would soon run out of wood for heating and cooking. In a few localities, operators signed temporary agreements at 60 cents per hour with May 6, 1935 as the starting date on final agreement. Pulp mills began to close as they ran out of chip supply.

The strike dragged on through May and June 1935 and mills began to reopen without a settlement, police and National Guard units were brought in to protect returning workers from violence. Longview operations resumed May 31, 1935 after 1000 union members voted 9-1 for acceptance of the original offer, of 5 cents an hour increase and a 40 hour work week. However union recognition was not granted and this would become a basis for further trouble. (18)

Repudiation of A. W. Muir and the Northwest Timber Workers Council became increasingly strident. On June 4, 1935, 500 delegates from striking union locals met in Aberdeen, Washington to set up a new strike organization, which had as its purpose, rejection of the Longview agreement. A 75 cent an hour minimum and union recognition was the objective. Also high on their list was the ouster of A. W. Muir. The new labor council was predominantly, made up of radical locals who felt that Muir and his group were too soft on the operators. (19)

On June 5, 1935, only a few days after returning to work, shingle weavers force the closure of the Longview operations, openly rebelling against A. W. Muir. The Shingle Weavers action surprised the lumber workers and was a solid indication that Muir's plan was not working. During the previous walkout, violence had not been a factor in the Longview area; but two members of the A.F. of L. council were beaten by gangs of men in Longview. A.W. Muir said that communists were the instigators of the beatings and encouraging the unrest. (20)

The Aberdeen council formed a joint strike committee of sawmill workers and shingle weavers. The committee gave notice that the parent union, A.F. of L., would no longer negotiate with the operators and any new negotiations would be on the original demands. A.W. Muir continued to aggressively promote his plan. The entire union movement was becoming divided, with Portland, Oregon and Bellingham, Washington locals, solidly behind Muir, while the rest were supporting the Aberdeen council. The Aberdeen council advised locals to hold back union dues from the parent union. With the strike committee in apparent control, A.W. Muir and the A.F. of L., struck back at opposing locals, by expelling leaders and locals who opposed his settlement. A.W. Muir also made sure the operators knew who the dissident leaders with communistic ties were, hoping to turn the trend back to more moderate course of action. (21)

Picketing increased at both Longview mills and the state patrol warned pickets to keep roads open. Aberdeen pickets fanned out across the Northwest to most all locations, to enforce the closures. With the strike now in the sixth week, locally loggers favor the Muir settlement, while the mill workers, shingle weavers, plywood workers and boom workers support the strike for higher pay. A.W. Muir served notice that he would revoke the charter of local 2504 for refusing to accept the negotiated settlement, claiming the strike was illegal and unauthorized. In mid June 1935, 87 pickets had been arrested for violating the no picketing rule and later tear gas was used to disperse strikers. The area around Longview was subject to many encounters with police and those who wished to return to work. Constant pressure from local and state police kept strikers from blocking roads into the mills. Muir continued to close locals and suspend members, pressing for acceptance of his contract. Eventually the tide began to turn against the Aberdeen strike committee and mills were returning to work. By late July 1935, the strike was about over. Pressure from Washington's governor, with assistance from state police, local law enforcement officers and the National Guard, all supported Muir's position. Although scattered picketing occurred, it was obvious that labor had enough of the strike.

The Longview local facing loss of the charter, after being expelled, refused to turn over the charter and local funds. The president and trustee resigned. A.W. Muir, having the full support of William Green, national president of A. F. of L, ordered the Longview local split into three separate units, one for each company and a separate local for the Weyerhaeuser woods operation.

The Long-Bell local was taken over by the strike committee resulting in more violence on the picket line. William Green ordered formal suspension of local 2504 and replaced with locals 2640, 2641 and 2642. The officers of local 2504 went to court to prevent the suspension and also, enjoined the state patrol from halting picketing.

On September 18, 1936 six hundred twenty five delegates from ten districts met in Portland, Oregon to discuss forming an industrial union. Representatives from logging and sawmill workers, plywood and veneer, pile drivers, coopers, shingle weavers, furniture, rafters and boom men were in attendance. The festering fight with A. W. Muir and the Carpenter and Joiners union grew uglier each week. The local unions strongly objected to the dictatorial methods of A. W. Muir and that the Carpenters and Joiners would only recognize the woodworkers union as fraternal brothers without voting rights within the Carpenters and Joiners union. The new group represented 72,000 wood workers, becoming the largest union organization on the West Coast. The new organization while not wanting to make a total break with the A. F. of L. insisted on changes that A. W. Muir and the parent union refused to make. At the national convention of Carpenters and Joiners, November 1936, sixteen delegates from the Federation of Woodworkers, asked for full voting rights on all lumber related matters. They were snubbed and the General Secretary, Frank Duffy, declared that the lumber workers were undesirable and if they dared to set up a separate union, they would get the fight of their lives. (22)

Ignored by the A. F. of L. carpenters and Joiners, the sixteen delegates went to Washington D. C. seeking an audience with John L. Lewis, who was actively developing the Industrial Workers union. The C. I. O. (Congress of Industrial Organization) workers consisted of the auto and steel industries. Due to limited funds and heavily engaged with the organizing efforts for the auto and steel workers, the delegates received little support.(23)

In June 1937 the Federation of Woodworkers, held a convention to consider affiliating with the C.I.O. and sent invitations to A. F. of L. president William Hutcheson to attend as well as John Brophy , C. I. O. director of organization and Harry Bridges, West Coast organizer of the Longshoremen's union. Hutcheson ignored the invitation and sent A. W. Muir instead, with Brophy and Bridges also there. The mood was definitely pro- C.I.O. With a defiant A. F. of L. president Hutcheson accusing the group as a pack of communists, the delegates decided on July 17, 1937 to join with the C.I.O.

Unable to persuade the dissident workers, back to the A. F. of L. membership, the A. F. of L. declared war. The Portland, Oregon, Tacoma and Bellingham/ Everett areas were battlegrounds with union members fighting each other. Battles were often brutal and bloody, with bombings, beatings and boycotts involved. It continued until the early 1940's before the last skirmish ended.

Locally, Long-Bell and Weyerhaeuser workers were able to avoid the violence and co-existed with A. F. of L. locals. With the affiliation in 1937 with the C. I. O., the Longview local chapter was designated as I. W. A.Local 5-36. Throughout the history of the I.W.A., the affiliation with leftist leaning philosophy caused all who were involved plenty of grief. The A.F. of L., timber operators and the U. S. Government were constantly attacking key leaders of the I.W.A. over supposed support of communistic principles.

The Longview labor situation saw long term labor peace, with the exception of strikes in 1948, and a summer long walkout in 1954. The C.I.O. slowly purged itself of left leaning leadership and moved toward a more conservative posture. Locally the Long-Bell and Weyerhaeuser workers fared far better than their counterparts at other locals. It would take many years, before the labor fraternity would cooperate and have trust in each other. Both Long-Bell and Weyerhaeuser exited the production of shingles in the late 1930's, due to often disruption by the shingle weavers union. It is ironic that the 4-L union lasted well into the 1940's despite labor and the U.S. Government efforts to eliminate the union as bargaining factor. The union was a factor in Eastern Washington and Northern Idaho mills.

References:

1) Nameless Towns Texas Sawmill Communities Thad Sitton/ James H. Conrad, Pages 113-114

2) Nameless Towns Texas Sawmill Communities Thad Sitton/ James H. Conrad, Page 122

3) Robert Alexander Long A Lumberman of a Gilded Age, Lenore K. Bradley, Page 67

4) Robert Alexander Long A Lumberman of a Gilded Age,   Lenore K. Bradley, Page 70

5) Board of Director Meeting Notes, September 17 1913

6) Siskiyou Pioneer Weed Edition, Union- Strikes- Aftermath,   Pages 77 to 85

7) Longview Daily News,   October 14, 1931, Pages 1 & 5

8) One Union in Wood,   Jerry Lembeke and William T. Tattam, Page 19

9) One Union in Wood,   Jerry Lembeke and William T. Tattam, Pages 30/31

10) Longview Daily News, June 27,1933, Page 7

11) Longview Daily News, July 11, 1933, Page 6

12) Longview Daily News, July 31, 1933, Pages 1 & 8

13) Longview Daily News, August 1, 1934, Page 1

14) Longview Daily News, March 15 1934, Page   1

15) Longview Daily News, April 13, 1935, Page 1 & 11

16) Longview Daily News, May 11, 1935,   Page 1 & 7

17) Longview Daily News, May 15, 1935,   Page 1 & 7

18) Longview Daily News, May 30, 1935, Page 1 & 7

19) Longview Daily News, June 4, 1935, Page 1 & 6

20) Longview Daily News, June 5, 1935, Page 1 & 9

21) Longview Daily News,   June 11, 1935, Page 5

22) One Union in Wood,   Jerry Lembeke and William T. Tattam,   Pages 43/44

23) One Union in Wood Jerry Lembeke and William T. Tattam Page 44

Chapter 18

PLYWOOD

Long-Bell's history is filled with innovative products required in the building trades and a key one is Plywood. The production of Plywood from its introduction in 1905, through World War II was primarily for specific or industrial end uses. Long-Bell entered into veneer production at Weed, CA. in 1906 for the box plant, producing veneer for box lids and bottoms. In 1911 the plant was converted to plywood production with construction of a small facility producing ponderosa and Sugar Pine door panels. The volume was approximately 10,000 sq. feet per day with the on grade panels sent to the door factory, (approximately 1000 doors per day) adjacent to the plywood plant. The lower quality veneer was sold to trunk and furniture plants for drawer sides and trunk bottoms. Plywood products other than door panels were sold by the Weed sales office, similar to sash and door and box shook. Long-Bell only sold the lumber items which were cut at Weed. This practice continued until 1917, when the company purchased complete control of the Weed operation. (1)

The plant increased in capacity in 1921 to 25,000 square feet per 8 hour shift, which fit the expansion of the Sash and Door department. The plywood production, except for the doors was sold through existing agents in Northern California, Wendling-Nathan and Homer Maris. (2) By 1940 it was decided to further expand the plant; but due to World War II, it would be   1948 before the expansion was completed, with production rated at 130,000 square feet per day. (3) At this point, the plant produced Douglas Fir panels as well as Ponderosa and Sugar Pine. In the last expansion, new equipment and innovations replaced much of the 20's type machinery. Block steaming (smoother peel), a new veneer tray system, a faster more efficient sander and a 16 opening press were installed. The lathe and dryers were also replaced, making the Weed plant one of the most up to date plants in the industry. The Weed plant operated until September 12, 1975.

Long-Bell continued its interest in plywood, with construction of a plant at Gardiner, Oregon, in 1950, with a capacity of 250,000 square feet per day (60 million feet 3/8 measure). The original intent was for the production to be sent to the Weed door plant. However the evolution of the plant turned toward sanded panels for concrete form, sidings and other high value products. In 1960 the Gardiner plant was expanded to reach 90 million feet 3/8 measure on an annual basis.

The capacity increase included the capability to produce 5x10 panels. The addition also changed product mix to include sheathing panels. (4)

In 1955, Long-Bell added its third plywood plant by purchasing the M@Mplywood plant located on the Long-Bell, Longview mill site. The plant produced mainly sanded panels with a small percentage of sheathing. This plant was built in 1929 and operated until1959/1960. The original agreement between Long-Bell and M@M was for Long-Bell to sell peeler logs to the plywood plant and have the ability to purchase panels for inclusion in their rail shipments. (5)In 1955, Long-Bell built a mill at the Vaughn, Oregon, complex with volume rated at 70 million feet 3/8 measure. The product mix was primarily sanded and had capacity for 9'and 10' panels along with the 4'x8' panels. (6) Long-Bell operated the plant until the early 1980's, when it was leased to Bohemia Lumber Company who operated it until the 1990's.

In 1960, as Long-Bell prepared to close the Longview plant site, a new facility was being constructed at Chelatchie Prairie, Washington. Long-Bell had obtained the timber rights on the south side of Mt St Helens in the upper Lewis River valley. The Chelatchie plant was built in conjunction with a sawmill and had a capacity of 72 million feet 3/8 measure annual production. Lathes capable of peeling 8',9' and 10' blocks were installed along with steam vats which Long-Bell had pioneered. The plant building (5 acres under roof) was the largest plywood facility built by Long-Bell. Production began July 1962, employing 250, and ran until 1979 . In an effort to improve profitability, the Chelatchie plant produced Hardwood faced panels as well as Douglas Fir, with Birch and Mahogany species being dominant. (7)

Sources

(1) Weed and Long-Bell, Published by The Plywood Pioneers Association, December 1967, Page 3

(2) Long-Bell Log, August 1920,   Page9 &10

(3) Weed and Long-Bell, Published by The Plywood Pioneers Association, December 1967, Page 6

(4) Weed and Long-Bell, Published by The Plywood Pioneers Association, December 1967, Page 6

(5) Weed and Long-Bell, Published by The Plywood Pioneers Association, December 1967, Page 6

(6) Weed and Long-Bell, Published by The Plywood Pioneers Association, December 1967, Page 6

(7) Long-Bell Log, March 1959 , Page 3 & 4

VENEER STREAMS from new ten-foot lathe peeling a Douglas fir block at Chelatchie. Lathe operator is Delbert Nelson. Note target pattern (right center) on end of peeler block held by automatic lathe charger.

Chapter 19

THE FAMILY

While forming and developing the growth of the Long-Bell Lumber Company, R. A. Long was most fortunate in associating with quality men of experience. Working relationships, formed during these early years, lasted throughout Mr. Long's life, and often encompassed more than one generation. The initial group of employees, were educated mainly through experience rather than formal schooling. As the company, grew exposure to the retail lumber and sawmill business through a variety of assignments, prepared them for greater responsibility and investment opportunities. Mr. Long's associates were generally divided between employees and investors; but often would be both an investor and employee.

The company was a firm believer in developing and promoting from within the organization. Entry into the company as a laborer, led to positions in the retail system or at the mill as a lumber grader, car line tallyman, shipping clerk, salesman onto mill superintendent and management. Few employees who moved into upper ranks of management had formal educations. Often starting work at 15 to16 years of age or younger, the company's method of training was so thorough and demanding that little was left out of the education process. (1)

Despite the occasional labor troubles of the early 1900's, R. A. Long often referred to the company employees as family. It has been noted in other portions of this book about the sorry state of living conditions and wages the southern mill employees had to contend with. Throughout the southern producing region, operators tended to treat labor rather poorly. Long-Bell was one of the better employers, adding extra amenities to the communities where they operated.

In all but a few locations, Long-Bell provided housing, community facilities, medical, electrical, schools, water and the company store. A company doctor and often two, provided health services to the mill and community. In some location dental care was available. Cost would be minimal. Southern locations required separate housing for black and white but also for Mexican, Greek or Japanese workers who normally worked the railroad construction. All employees used the company store but all other facilities would be segregated. Company sponsored baseball and basketball teams would compete with local teams in surrounding areas, fostering a sense of community.

Long-Bell practiced safety habits throughout the organization for many years. The Long-Bell Log often carried articles concerning safe working habits and practices to encourage safety. The use of eye protection was promoted for those working around saws. In the early years of the 20th century, pay check stubs carried safety messages, helping to carry the message into the workers home and family. Accident prevention was used in competition between the various mill operations in order to promote safe working conditions. (2)

Long-Bell had definite policies in place to take care of salaried employees in the case of extended illness or death. In the event of death of a salaried employee, the Board of Directors would usually extend the salary at half pay to the widow and family for one year.

Common labor rates were seldom more than $1.50 to $2.00 per day during the early years of 1900, evidence of voluntary increases in daily rates occurred during periods of strong markets. Arbitrary increases in salaried positions were reported in Board of Director notes, initiated by Mr. Long. Vacations were encouraged among salaried personnel, although it is not clear if vacations were paid by the company. The period during World War I was the most active for wage increases.

Evidence, that protections for the laboring class were forthcoming, was through passage of a workman's compensation act by the Louisiana Legislature in 1914. Provisions to offer accident protection, were built into the act after a two week waiting period. Many mill operators, including Long-Bell offered insurance coverage for the two week waiting period at a minimal cost. A significant movement toward protection of the labor force. Other states quickly followed with similar legislation. (4)

In Long-Bell's rich history, the longevity of the work force and the successive generations who worked for the company stand out. It seems that once a family member worked for the company, there was always an opportunity for others in the family to obtain work. The company history is replete with stories of long time employment with an amazing roster of employees who had 50 years of service with the company. R. A. Long was able to surround himself with a core of outstanding men who had the ability to get things done, had long term vision, with little formal education.

A review of the "Long-Bell Log" which recorded length of service, in five year increments, would publish monthly the names of employees who reached another milestone. The listings printed below should be considered as minimums, as the "Log" did not publish from 1930 through 1938. The records show 22 employees with 50 years or more of service, 27 with 45 plus years, 90 with 40 plus years, 140 with 35 plus years, 103 with 30 plus years, and 170 with 25 or more years of service. This sample works out to 18, 155 years of service to Long-Bell.

The "Log" was published by the company, to inform the employees about individuals, families of employees, sports teams, promotions and items of general interest. Many articles about the movement and growth of the company to the Northwest also included items of local interest, such as Spirit Lake and Mount Saint Helens, Mt. Rainier and the Columbia River. Many employees were asked to move and the "Log" was used to educate them about the new country where they were going to move.

Until social security became mature enough so that a worker could retire, with some sense of stability, there was not an age when one retired. One worked until job performance was no longer satisfactory. Many employees worked well past the age of 65 and often workers were in their 70's and 80's, still employed. An article in the May 2, 1928 edition of The Longview Daily News wrote of a logger at Ryderwood who resigned at age 82. Jess Tucker, a former shipping clerk at Calcasieu Lumber Company, Lake Charles, LA., was employed at the East Mill Shipping Department, Longview, well into his 80's. Many other examples exist where the company continued to employ people well past the normal retirement age. Injured or handicapped employees were also taken care of where possible.

At Southern locations, workers were split between black and white, generally 50/50%, depending on mill location. Housing was provided but segregated. At Weed, CA. the population was split into three separate living areas. The white population with the exception of the Italian's, were in one section, Italians in a second area and Blacks and Hispanics in the third section. Blacks came to Weed in 1918 but the majority came in 1922 as a result of a strike and by 1925 over 1000 lived in the area and worked at the mill.

When Longview was developed, blacks were not hired at the mill, although several families lived in the community. The Longview mill did have a contingent of Japanese (38 employees) who manned the green chains quite effectively. They were very loyal employees until forced to move in mid 1942, to relocation camps. They were universal in purchasing War Bonds for the coming war effort. The employees and their families lived next to the West mill Shipping sheds in a segregated community.(5) There was also a large contingent of Japanese workers at the Longville, Louisiana plant and their main function was track maintenance.

Long-Bell had good relations with its work force, despite the occasional strike. At a meeting with The Loyal Legion of Loggers and Lumbermen (The existing union prior to the depression), R. A. Long stated the following policy of the company, August 1922.:" It has been the policy of The Long-Bell Lumber Company for nearly 50 years to deal fairly with all men and we believe that the number of employees who have been in our service for twenty or thirty year periods is our best recommendation to the workers of the Northwest that we will make an honest effort to work harmoniously with them. Our company is entirely directed by men who have   risen from humble places within our organization. The managers of tomorrow are holding minor jobs today. This is our policy. We do not go outside for supervisors. We look around at home and do everything we can to train our men so they will climb to responsibility. Our big interests in the years to come will be located in the Northwest. Men and managers will find The Long-Bell Lumber Company working with them for all the things which, as men, we hold dear." The statement was published in the Four L Bulletin, August 1922.

When considering the longevity of the work force, it was evident that management cared about the employees and the employees appreciated management. It was normal to be recognized by senior company officials when they were visiting a plant site, knowing the individuals name and often what they did and how long they had worked for the company. It certainly makes the process of working for the same goals easier.

References:

(1) Long-Bell Log, August 1922, Page 21

(2) Long-Bell Log, January 1921, Page 8

(3) The Siskiyou Pioneer The Weed Edition Siskiyou County Historical Society, Page 32/38

(4) Board of Director Meeting Notes, January 12, 1915

(5) Internal Company Document , 1938

Chapter 20

JOHN DOUGLAS " J.D." TENANT

R. A. Long employed many talented men in building the Long-Bell Lumber Company. A strong believer of developing from within, his managers came from a broad background of experiences. All would prove proficient in the lumber trade, from retail through manufacturing and sales. In Long-Bell's long history, three men stand out as lieutenants to R. A. Long, M.B. "Mike" Nelson, J. D. Tennant and C. E. Lombardi. Mike Nelson was general sales manager for many years and became president of Long-Bell from 1921 until 1948. He was a right hand man to R.A. Long for many years and led the company through the roughest period in its history. C.E. Lombardi was chief counsel for the company and steered the company through the difficult financial crisis in the mid 1930's. However, J.D. Tenant was the public face of the company and would become a legend in the Lumber trade. John Douglas Tennant was the manufacturing manager for all of Long-Bell operations and upon purchasing the tract of timber in Washington State, became Western Manager for the company, responsible for building the Longview complex.

In 1898, Tennant joined Long-Bell in a minor position at Hudson River Lumber Company, Hudson, Arkansas, moving to De Ridder, Louisiana, in 1903/ 1904. He left to operate a retail yard at Independence, Kansas until 1906. He then moved to Lake Charles, Louisiana, to be order clerk at Calcasieu Lumber Company and in 1907, became General Superintendent at De Ridder until 1910, resigning to engage in the retail lumber business. In 1911, he returned to Long-Bell as assistant to C. B. Sweet, vice president of lumber manufacture for Long-Bell. In 1914, he was appointed vice president of manufacturing for Long-Bell and the associated companies and elected a director of the company. (1)

With the acquisition of the Washington timberlands and the decision to build a major complex at the confluence of the Cowlitz and Columbia rivers, J.D. Tennant was the man in charge of the operation. He reviewed the new timber stand, active in selecting the site for the town and the development of Longview. As the mill units moved toward completion, he was also given the responsibility for the Pine operations at Weed, California, and the Southern Oregon Timberland. The logging town for the Weed operation was named Tennant in his honor.

Long-Bell would become very active in industry affairs and J.D. Tenant would become the main company spokesman. With the formation of the West Coast Lumberman's Association, which was a combination, of the West Coast Grading Bureau and the product promotion group, Tennant would be named president in 1927 and remain as president and director until 1933. During the serious depression period, lumber markets were a disaster, with shortened hours and layoffs rampant. The new administration of Franklin Roosevelt initiated many programs in an attempt to put men back to work. One of these programs, The National Recovery Act, created a series of codes, which controlled the volume, hours worked, minimum wages and minimum prices that products could be sold. J.D. Tennant was selected as chairman of the National Code Authority for Lumber and related products, representing over 36,000 operations, employing 3 to400,000 workers.

Tennant was an ideal choice, having been involved with Southern Pine, Western and Ponderosa Pine operations. He was well respected throughout the industry. He would remain chairman of the Code Authority until it dissolved in 1935, due lack of federal enforcement over code violations.

In 1931 Tennant and R.H. Barr (a local logger of timber on the Coweeman River in Cowlitz County) formed a logging venture at Stevenson, Washington, to log 235 million feet of Douglas Fir timber. Long-Bell would be a major recipient of the saw timber. In 1938, he was elected President of Ochoco Timber Company, Prineville, Oregon, a Ponderosa Pine Lumber Company where R. A. Long had made a substantial investment. He carried this task along with his Long-Bell duties until he retired in 1948.

Tennant was very active in the local community of Longview, Washington, being the first president of the local hospital association, now Peace Health. He was an early Y.M.C.A. board member, also active, in the formation of Lower Columbia College. He was a director of Longview Fiber Company, with whom Long-Bell had a major investment and a long term raw material contract over the life of the mill complex. He also served as director of the Western Pine and Southern Pine Associations.

John D. Tennant served Long-Bell and the Lumber Industry for 48 years, most of it in major roles in the development of the company. Well known throughout the industry and government circles, he served with distinction. Born December 30, 1882 in Lanaconing, Maryland, he died April 14, 1949 after an illness of 9 months. R.A. Long could not have asked for a better Lieutenant in the development of the company.

References:

(1) Long-Bell Log, July 1924, Page 8

(2) Longview Daily News, February 10, 1928, Page 1

(3) Longview Daily News, July 1, 1933, Page 1

(4) Longview Daily News, July 8, 1931, Page 1

(5) Ochco Big Pine Country, Rick Steber, Bonanza Publications, Prineville, Oregon,

Pages 51, 52 and 56

(6) Longview Daily News, April 14, 1949, Page 1

Chapter 21

THE END

With the merging of Long-Bell assets into International Paper starting in 1956, the identity of the company began to fade. For several years, other than changing letterheads and signs at mill locations the general public was not aware that a change had been made. However as senior management began to retire, new faces came into the company. International Paper while continuing to support the Long-Bell division with capital dollars for new plant construction at Vaughan, Gardiner and Chelatchie Prairie, soon began to absorb administrative function into the parent company. With the closing of the Longview operation, the sales and marketing function moved to Portland, Oregon.

International Paper maintained a major presence in the Western producing region until the 1980s, when economic conditions similar to our present situation (2012), necessitated wholesale closures of all wood products locations. International Paper would continue to hold extensive acreage of timberland and a pulp mill at Gardiner, Oregon but would be out of the wood products business in the west.

Long-Bell management developed a first class company, becoming the largest producer of lumber in the 1920's, pioneering in treated products, expanding into sash, doors and window products to give them entry in markets few others could compete. Hardwoods were a natural added product line making the company the second largest producer in the industry. The addition of Oak Flooring gave the company a tremendous boost in their marketing efforts.

From the very beginnings of the company, the purchasing of lumber from other sources was important to the success of the company. Quickly the purchases of lumber products lead to the establishment of field sales offices. This was done to keep a steady flow of product from contract mills, while allowing the company to expand product volume into more markets. The expansion allowed Long-Bell to have markets ready for their own mills as they came on line. Having the foresight to provide products other than Southern Pine tended to draw customers closer to the company. In the eighteen years the company operated a purchasing office and concentration yard in Tacoma, Washington from 1894 to 1912, they purchased averaged 1600 carloads a year of lumber and shingles. It was stated company policy that mill production was not to be dedicated to the retail system unless there was not any other alternative. In the 1920's, 40 to 45 million feet of wood products were being purchased and would increase after the depression was over.

In addition to finished product, purchases of rough and finished lumber were made at the local mill level. Cedar Bevel Siding was a key item needed in mixed car shipments and Long-Bell purchased these items in volume from specialty mills. It was noted that the Longview mill shipped 60 million feet of purchased items during their record year 1941, when a total of 510 million feet was loaded.

The company affected thousands of lives with several generations of a family working for the company. Promoting from within gave many employees opportunities that might not have happened elsewhere. The company sought to be firm; but fair with their employees, seldom paying wages that were not average or above the scale. Once someone in a family worked for Long-Bell, there was always the opportunity for the rest.

Long-Bell should have been able to produce lumber for several years longer than they did; but financial trouble of the early 1930's destroyed the opportunity. Canceling a major timber contract with Weyerhaeuser for Lewis and Cowlitz County acreage was a major blow. The tract was purchased in 1928. Also a contract for a sizeable tract of Ponderosa Pine in Modoc County, California, was cancelled. Both tracts would have added years to the life of the mills involved.

Long-Bell and later International Paper would play a significant role in manufacture and distribution of lumber, plywood, treated products, doors, windows, hardwoods, oak flooring and many other products. In the 105 years that the company was in existence, the impact on the wood products trade was tremendous. Unfortunately few people today would ever know they were in business. During their long history, the company produced in excess of 30 billion feet of lumber.

Southern Pine/Hardwoods	11.355 billion feet	1898-1962
Weed/ Southern Oregon	6.635 billion feet	1902-1980
Western Mills	12.366 billion feet	1924-1980

In addition to the lumber produced, treated products in the millions of pieces, thousands of doors and windows and boxes, billions of feet of plywood and the myriad of products flowing through the retail chain. Long-Bell played a major role in the expansion and settlement of the United States, especially the Southwest.

Today the massive mill structures at Longview and elsewhere are gone and the mills but a memory. To the citizens of Longview, Weed, Yellow Pine, DeRidder and other mill locations, belongs the knowledge that products they produced, helped build the country in a time of rapid growth. For the many thousands of employees, who worked for Long-Bell and their leaders, a job well done.

Chapter 22

PROFITABILITY/ LOSS

Listed below is a chronological profit or loss record for Long-Bell. The figures listed are net earnings from annual reports or documents uncovered during a search for historical facts about the company. The years 1939 and 1940 we were unable to locate any information. The period listed is from 1913 through 1955. Long-Bell merged with International Paper in 1956.

Year	Amount	Year	Amount
1913	$ 1,054,000.	1938	$ 537,549.
1914	$ 484,000.	1939	NA
1915	$ 437,000.	1940	NA
1916	$ 2,130,000.	1941	$ 2,989,167.
1917	$ 3,559,000.	1942	$ 2,295,000.
1918	$ 2,169,000.	1943	$ 152,692.
1919	$ 4,439,000.	1944	$ 1,947,771.
1920	$ 5,772,000.	1945	$ 1,732,897.
1921	$ 80,000.	1946	$ 4,985,390.
1922	$ 4,334,000.	1947	$12,660,683.
1923	$ 5,659,000.	1948	$12,699,859.
1924	$ 4,006,000.	1949	$ 6,969,947.
1925	$ 4,812,000.	1950	$ 11,084,807.
1926	$ 2,718,000.	1951	$ 8,614,268.
1927	$ 1,498,000.	1952	$ 6,281,360.
1928	$ 1,936,000.	1953	$ 5,489,387.
1929	$ 1,659,000	1954	$ 3,748,107

1930	($ 3,736,000.)	1955	$ 9,730,463.
1931	($ 7,972,000.)		
1932	($ 5,015,552.)		
1933	($ 3,685,207.)		
1934	($ 9,000,000.)		
1935	($ 464,519.)		
1936	$ 419,371.		
1937	$ 999,163.		

References: Long-Bell Financial Statements and C. R. Cornwall report

Chapter 23

A LISTING OF SAWMILLS OPERATED BY LONG-BELL 1880- 1981

Long-Bell was involved in operating mills, financing mills or purchasing all, or a portion of the production to service their Retail Yards and Wholesale operations. The following list represents their involvement in Southern Pine, West Coast and Ponderosa Pine mills.

Date Started Mill Name	Location	Date Closed
1889 Barnes Lumber	Van Buren, Arkansas	1896
1889 Barnes Lumber	Pea Ridge, Arkansas	1896
1889 Barnes Lumber	Drake, Arkansas	1896
1890 King/ Ryder Lbr.	Antlers, Indian Territory	1894
1895 James L. McCoy Lbr.	Horatio, Arkansas	1901
1895 Whited@Wheless Lbr.	Alden Bridge, Arkansas	1903/1904
1895 Gifford Lumber	Gifford, Arkansas	1898 / 1903
1895 Junction City Lbr.	Junction City, Arkansas	1902
1897 Malvern Lumber	Perla, Arkansas	1903
1897 Klondike Lumber	Winthrop, Arkansas	1904/1905
1897 Rapides Lumber	Woodworth, Louisiana	1926
1898 Hudson Lumber	Hudson, Arkansas	1902
1898 Globe Lumber	Yellow Pine, Louisiana	1913
1900 R. L. Trigg Lumber	Noble, Louisiana	1910
1901 King-Ryder Lumber	Bon Ami, La	1925
1902 Hudson River Lumber	De Ridder, Louisiana	1960's
1904 Weed Lumber	Weed, California	1981
1905 Stearns Lumber	Wendling, California	1920 / 1922
1905 Lufkin Land and Timber	Lufkin Texas	1930
1906 Calcasieu Longleaf Lbr.	Lake Charles, Louisiana	1928

1906 Calcasieu Longleaf Lbr.	Mt. Holly, Louisiana	1908/1910
1907 Hardy Lumber Company	Location Unknown	
1907 Longville Lumber	Longville, Louisiana	1923*
1911 Arkansas Short Leaf Lbr.	Pine Bluff, Arkansas	1922*
1912 Thompson- Tucker Lbr.	Willard, Texas	1913/1914
1912 Thompson- Tucker Lbr.	Trinity, Texas	1913/1914
1912 Fidelity Lumber	Doucette, Texas	1945**
1913 Ludington Lumber	Ludington, Louisiana	1926
1913 Long-Bell	Pine Bluff, Arkansas	1928
1917 Long-Bell	Quitman/Crandall, Mississippi	1963
1923 Long-Bell	Longview, Washington	1961
1923 Long-Bell	Wilmott, Arkansas	1924
1928 Superior Oak Flooring	Helena, Arkansas	1930
1935 Shaw Lumber	Klamath Falls, Oregon	1942
1936 Kesterson Lumber	Dorris, California	1945
1938 Ochoco Lumber	Prineville, Oregon	1950/1951
1944 Long-Bell	Sheridan, Arkansas	1960'S
1945 Snellstrom Lumber	Vaughan, Oregon	1981
1947 Austa Lumber	Austa, Oregon	1970'S
1948 Gardiner Lumber	Gardiner, Oregon	1980
1950 Etna Lumber	Etna, California	1960/1970'S
1953 Oregon American Lumber	Vernonia, Oregon	1957
1960 Huff Lumber	Scotts Valley, California	1965/1966
1963 International Paper	Chelatchie Prairie,Washington	1979

- These two mills were destroyed by fire.

- ** Fidelity Lumber was also part of The Thompson-Tucker, Long-Bell dispute.

Forty Four separate facilities over a seventy five year span, with a distinct possibility of others.

GLOSSARY

Air Drying — Piled lumber with separation between each course to allow air flow through, reducing the moisture content

Blanks — Lumber which is surfaced two sides; but not edges, designed to be rerun to pattern.

Boom* — A raft of logs or lumber held in the water.

Black List — A do not hire list due to perceived union activity.

Box Shook — Sawn and surfaced lumber used in the production of wooden boxes.

Butt* — The bottom of the tree. The stump end of a log.

Cut Stock — Surfaced and trimmed lumber of various lengths used in the production of windows, doors and industrial wood parts.

Cant — A sawn section of a log, designed for further manufacture.

C. C. C. — Civilian Conservation Corp, a public works program established during the depression of the 1930's. Established for single men 18 to 26, who were the most vulnerable in the job market during this period of time. The work was mostly forestry and conservation oriented and organized on a military regimen.

Clyde Loader and Skidder* — A self propelled steam skidder used in early railroad logging.

Distribution Yard — A bulk storage facility of wood products for resale

Dry Kiln — Mechanical drying of lumber through controlled heat, air and steam.

Carriage Dogs — Device to hold the log on to the saw carriage.

Donkey Engine* — An endless variety of steam, gas, diesel or electric power plants, plus drums to hold wire rope, all used to haul/ load or move logs.

Drop Sorter — Mechanical lumber sorter by length.

Door Patterns — Variety of styles available in the production of doors.

Finger Joint — Mechanical process to allow inter locking of lumber to utilize short lengths.

High Wheels* — A woods cart with large wheels used to haul logs.

Head Rig — Location of the main saw which cuts the logs into lumber, cants or flitches which would be futher manufactured.

I.T.	Indian Territory
Fbm	Feet board measure
Jilpoke*	A stout pole used in shoving loaded log cars from a spur to the main line track
Lath	It is a product of slabs or edgings from the head mill in sizes 5/16" or ½" one inch to one and one half inches wide 48" inches long. It is a byproduct of the sawmill and was used in the interior of homes that were plastered.
O.T.	Oklahoma Territory
Line Yards	A group of retail yards owned by one entity.
Retail Yard struction.	A store designed to sell lumber, plywood, and other related products used in con-
M	One thousand board feet.
M M	One million board feet.
Naval Stores	Terpentine, Rosin and other products obtained from the sap or pitch of a pine tree.
Flitch the log.	A sawn portion of the log, designed for remanufacture. Usually on the outside of
Railroad Spur	A railroad siding which went into the logging area.
Shotgun Rig	The log carriage which carries the log through the saw, powered by steam.
Shipping Clerk	Responsible person who organizes the loading of lumber orders.
Plywood 3/8" Equivalent	
	Plywood is sold on square footage basis but measured for statistical purposes us ing 3/8' as a base point. The same as lumber being measured on a board foot basis.
Peeler Block	The section of the log which is peeled to make veneer.
Shop Lumber	Lumber, produced with defects such as large knots, to be cut out, developing clear sections for further manufacture.
Service Station	A distribution yard.
Steam Vaults	Heated chambers for conditioning Plywood blocks. The result of the steaming makes for a smoother peel.
Sash and Door	Window frame and door production and sale.
Refuse Burner	Disposal chamber for edgings and trimmings used in mills for waste disposal, prior to the 1950's.

Window Glazing	Placing and sealing glass in window frames.
Window Lights	Window openings.
Union Shop	A workplace that has a union with collective bargaining rights. It is not mandatory to join a union in this type of shop.
Talley Man	The worker who counts the lumber being loaded for shipment, or being assembled for loading.
Turnover	The number of times inventory will move in a given time period.
I.W.W/ Wobblies*	A member of the Industrial Workers of The World, or other radical labor movement.

* All entries with an asterisk were selected from the publication Woods Words Walter F. McCoulloch 1977 Oregon State University Book Store Inc. Corvallis, Oregon. The other entries are those of the author.

INDEX

Made in the USA
San Bernardino, CA
30 January 2015